TOLARNO
Bistro

TOLARNO

The life, times and recipes
of a remarkable restaurant

IAIN HEWITSON AND BOB HART
Photography by Greg Elms

First published in 2006

Copyright recipes © Iain Hewitson 2006
Copyright text © Bob Hart 2006
Copyright photography © Greg Elms 2006

All rights reserved. No part of this book may be reproduced or transmitted in any form or by any means, electronic or mechanical, including photocopying, recording or by any information storage or retrieval system, without prior permission in writing from the publisher. The *Australian Copyright Act 1968* (the Act) allows a maximum of one chapter or 10% of this book, whichever is greater, to be photocopied by any educational institution for its educational purposes provided that the educational institution (or body that administers it) has given remuneration to Copyright Agency Limited (CAL) under the Act.

Allen & Unwin
83 Alexander Street
Crows Nest NSW 2065
Australia
Phone: (61 2) 8425 0100
Fax: (61 2) 9906 2218
Email: info@allenandunwin.com
Web: www.allenandunwin.com

National Library of Australia
Cataloguing-in-publication entry:
    Hewitson, Iain.
    Tolarno Bistro : the life, time and recipes of a remarkable restaurant.

    1st ed.
    Includes index.
    ISBN 978 1 74114 956 2.

    ISBN 1 74114 956 8.

    1. Tolarno Bistro. 2. Restaurants - Victoria - St. Kilda - History. I. Hart, Bob. II. Title.

    647.959451

Research by Ruth Krawat
Designed and typeset by Phil Campbell
Food styled by Virginia Dowzer
Edited by Megan Johnston
Index by Fay Donlevy
Printed in Singapore by Imago
10 9 8 7 6 5 4 3 2 1

The author and publisher wish to thank Empire III Vintage, Ladelle and Market Import for their generous loan of dinnerware and napery used in the food photography.
www.empirevintage.com.au
www.ladelle.com.au
marketimport@bigpond.com

This book is dedicated to Mirka and Georges Mora,
Leon and Vivienne Massoni, David Gibson, Ruth Allen
and all the wonderful staff, suppliers and customers
who made Tolarno such a vibrant, exciting,
fun establishment over so many years.

Thank you for all the good times.

Contents

Introduction — viii
Bistro, bistro — 2

The Mora Years — 5

Hors d'oeuvres, charcuterie and breads — 17
Some debatable history — 40
Entrees & soups — 47

The Massoni Years — 79

Poultry — 87
From the sea — 103
Lamb, veal and bits & pieces — 127

The Hewitson–Allen Years — 151

Beef & pork — 163
Salads & vegetables — 187

A day in the life of Tolarno — 215

Desserts — 225

End of an Era — 250

Basics — 253
Index — 260
Picture credits — 264

Introduction

Great restaurants are said to reflect and reconfirm the tastes, the attitudes and the lifestyles of those who choose to frequent them.

Tolarno French Bistro, later to become, at the time of our national displeasure with the French and their nuclear pursuits in the Pacific, simply Tolarno Bistro, has always been at least one jump ahead: for four decades, it has shaped the tastes, reinforced the attitudes and illuminated the lives of its patrons.

Tolarno began operating late in 1964 – at a time when restaurants in particular, and food in general, played less significant roles in the lives of Melburnians than either of them play today. The food revolution was under way, clearly, with some seriously-intentioned tucker – some of it of great formality and some of it French – on offer. But none of it, apart from the Tolarno offerings, came as part of a cultural program.

There was good Italian food to be found in the city at places like Florentino and The Society, The Latin and Mario's, and a few others. Serious restaurants, these – run by families that became known, affectionately, as the Spaghetti Mafia, indelibly inscribing names like Triaca, Vigano, Codognotto, Virgona, Molino, Massoni and others onto the pages of our culinary history. Other Italian names – most notably, perhaps, those of Gobbo, and of chefs Grossi and Catelli and others – belonged to families that busied themselves around the fringes and, ultimately, achieved their own inscriptions.

Half-decent Chinese food, also, was on offer in the city – extravagantly flavoured dishes, by the standards of the day, which adventurous but unworldly Melburnians were inclined to order by number, but enjoyed just the same. Generally, these were offered in less 'serious' restaurants – in one of which, called Wing Sun, a young Chinese student by the name of Gilbert Lau worked as a waiter, having memorised all the important numbers from the menu, including the prawn chop suey and the chicken chow mein. Gilbert remembered to remain expressionless rather than actually unenthusiastic when a patron ordered chicken maryland with dim sims or sweet and sour pork with chips, favourites of the day. He had already begun to dream of the day when he might own a restaurant of his own which he might or might not call Flower Drum, and which was destined, through its brilliance, to change the rules of engagement. But that, of course, is another story...

French bistro food – lubricated with dark wines, sometimes eaten in the company of loose women and/or loose men and alive with garlic and butter and life and decadence and authenticity and quite possibly, in the minds of at least some of the city's more ethnocentric citizens, garden snails, the limbs of amphibians and other unspeakable things – was quite another matter. Melbourne had still to be convinced that there was an approach to French food other than that taken by the likes of Maxim's, the increasingly opulent French restaurant which was run with great flair by Vincent Rosales in Toorak Road, and Antonio's in Greville Street, Prahran, where the incomparable Hermann Schneider was offering mousse of foie gras, champagne sorbets to cleanse the palate, and the like.

Tolarno creators Georges and Mirka Mora had, for early adopters of the more accessible bistro approach, provided a route through the garlic curtain with Café Balzac, the seminal French bistro they had opened in 1958 in Wellington Street, East Melbourne. Melburnians went to Balzac in droves and discovered, as many had secretly suspected, that there was rather more to eating out than ravioli and spring rolls, better conditions under which to enjoy a meal than the bleak solemnity of drab hotel dining rooms, and a less formal approach to French food than the silver cloches and ornate, gilt mirrors of Maxim's and Antonio's might have indicated.

International visitors, even French ones, adored Balzac: the eternally youthful Maurice Chevalier, as a sprightly septuagenarian, lunched there daily during a season of appearances at Spring Street's Princess Theatre and found great comfort in the food, the atmosphere, and the sublime company of Balzac's resident enchantress, Mirka, with whom he liked to share a pre-prandial stroll, daily, through Fitzroy Gardens.

But it was not until the Moras abandoned comparatively staid East Melbourne to move to raunchy St Kilda and opened Tolarno French Bistro in their expansive home in Fitzroy Street, the Tolarno Hotel, that Melbourne's conversion to the charms, the insouciance and the aromas of a genuine French bistro was complete. While Café Balzac continued without the Moras, much later flourishing under the stewardship of Florentino heir and future Tolarno operator Leon Massoni, Tolarno French Bistro offered a seductive mix of racy French dishes, determined bohemianism, fine art and debauched artists – all of it enhanced by the art and glorious eccentricities of Mirka and consolidated by the charm, elegance, generosity of spirit and supreme professionalism of Georges. And all of it unfolding in a part of town where, as it happened, prostitution was more deeply entrenched and more enthusiastically practised than gastronomy.

It is a sign of those times, perhaps, and an indication of prevailing attitudes, that one of the first news reports of Tolarno's existence failed to mention either the name of the restaurant or, indeed, the name of its predecessor, Café Balzac, to which it referred simply as a 'French restaurant in East Melbourne'. Tolarno, in that prominent report in *The Herald*, Melbourne's evening broadsheet, on 28 November 1964, was referred to simply as 'a new French bistro in Fitzroy St, St Kilda, serving only Parisian style food (so there'll be no strong garlic flavour or aroma)'. Well, not much, anyway.

The breathless report, by-lined Rachel Irvine, carried a prominent photograph of early chef Alain Guerin, a recently arrived Parisian who, as a fourth-generation French master-of-the-stoves, might have been alarmed to read the garlic disclaimer. In that photograph, a handsomely attired Guerin, resplendent beneath a white toque, piles hors d'oeuvres onto a plate to the apparent delight of head waitress Joly Ember, a Hungarian, in 'St Kilda's new French Bistro'. No name, no precise address. And no garlic, thank you. We're Anglo-Celtic.

Today, restaurants are named, discussed, celebrated and, at times, ferociously and even inexpertly criticised in newspapers. Such coverage, it is accepted, helps to sell those newspapers. But in 1964, in line with editorial attitudes of the day, the inclusion of a restaurant's name in such a report would have constituted free advertising, and could have made it all too easy for readers of *The Herald* to find the place and, quite possibly, to expose themselves to unimaginable temptations and other dangers.

Which most Melburnians – fortunately for the Moras, for subsequent operators of the business, for the health of our food and restaurant cultures and for future generations – were most anxious to do. They managed to find Tolarno French Bistro in darkest St Kilda without the direct assistance of *The Herald*, and gleefully exposed themselves to some very welcome peril.

And they have been finding the place, effortlessly, ever since. And living, in most cases, to tell the tale ...

Bistro, bistro

There is much debate about the origins of the word 'bistro'. Many feel that it was introduced into the French vocabulary by the Russians after they seized Paris in 1815. Supposedly, as they entered Parisian cafés, they would shout 'bystro, bystro' which, loosely translated, means 'quickly, quickly'.

Not everyone agrees with that explanation, however. The French – who hate to give credit to any other nation for contributing to a French word or expression (and that includes 'le hot dog', which, they will insist, is clearly of French derivation) – feel that the word comes from the northern slang term 'bistouille' which refers to a mix

of coffee and eau de vie – a concoction which, I have no doubt, has been consumed on a regular basis throughout the bistros of France.

But whatever its etymology, the bistro, in its purest form, was always a neighbourhood establishment – a place without pretensions where the locals gathered, a place they were able to treat almost as an extension of their kitchens or living rooms.

And in the life of Tolarno (French) Bistro, this has always been the spirit of the place: never expensive, rarely complicated. And the regulars, many of them local, have always been the core of the business and, as such, part of the Tolarno family.

Some poetic licence has been used in presenting the recipes in this book. Certainly, many of the favourite dishes from the Mora and Massoni eras have been included and, hopefully, my versions will deliver results that are similar to the originals.

But I have also included a number of French bistro classics which may or may not have appeared on Mora or Massoni menus. Obviously, I was not there for every menu change and, therefore, I cannot be sure that these recipes are for dishes that were actually served at Tolarno. Although I have my suspicions ...

During the Hewitson–Allen era, the menu did, at the behest of the patrons, move away from being purely French. But what never changed was the bohemian spirit of Tolarno and the sense that one was ensconced in one's own living room.

The MORA Years

The year was 1964 and Georges Mora was a desperate man. The Moras needed a family home – a place large and flexible enough to accommodate one artistic and deliciously eccentric wife, three precocious sons, a brace of cats, a bistro, an art gallery, the occasional visiting, inevitably destitute and often inebriated artist and, ideally, himself. And he was beginning to doubt that such a place existed in Melbourne. Or anywhere else in the civilised world, for that matter.

Georges felt as though he had looked at every property worthy of genteel inhabitation in the suburbs of South Yarra, Toorak, East Melbourne and beyond, testing the patience of the city's leading pedlars of real estate. Many of the places viewed had appealed enormously to Georges, and to his sons, and he happily would have closed a deal on several. But none of them – not a single one – appealed to the spirited and singular Mirka. Not even close, apparently.

'They were lovely, all of them. But I could not have lived in any of them,' she now explains. 'None of them, you see, had a studio. And without a studio, how can any painter live? Georges would plead with me to focus on the houses and to stop thinking only about a studio, but how could I possibly do that? It was out of the question.'

Eventually, Georges stopped looking, but kept an ear to the ground. And one day, in 1964, he arrived home with news that would shape the lives of his family, help to rehabilitate the suburb of St Kilda and, in time, enliven the dining and drinking habits of Melburnians. Georges had pulled off a masterstroke of which even the Mora cats, Napoleon and Stiffy – the former named for his bossiness, the latter because he was seldom without an erection, according to Mirka – would approve.

'Georges walked in and said he hoped I would be happy now: he had bought the Tolarno Hotel and, before I could even ask, he told me that yes, I could have a studio there, and the boys could have a room each, and that there was plenty of room for everything else we had ever wanted. Including, of course, a bistro, which we both wanted, and an art gallery for Georges,' says Mirka.

The family, on the whole, responded well to the surprising news. Only William, the eleven-year-old second-oldest of the three Mora sons, had a serious and testing question.

'Does it have a lift?' he asked his father. It did not, he was told. William was not entirely happy about this as he had long dreamed of living in a residence with a lift but, given the other advantages, he decided to make the best of things. For the moment.

↑ The artist's studio upstairs at Tolarno—Mirka at work with Georges and their three sons

Mirka, with her paints, her canvases and her head full of fanciful images, was moved into handsome space on the ground floor of the old hotel. But she was quickly evicted from there when Georges realised the space would make an even better gallery than an artist's studio, which it did – the Tolarno Gallery, in fact.

'I didn't really mind because I was moved upstairs into a bridal room, and I liked that very much,' giggles Mirka.

'Actually,' confides William, 'it wasn't a bridal room at all. It was a large room, but it was in the old part of the hotel and did not have an ensuite. I think Georges told her it was a bridal room to cheer her up. But she loved it anyway and produced some wonderful paintings in it.'

Downstairs, however, there was more serious work to be done, starting with the construction of a commercial kitchen to service the front room of the hotel – the room destined to become Tolarno French

Bistro – in which, to that point, only basic breakfasts, teas and coffees had ever been served for hotel guests. One or two of whom, incidentally, came with the acquisition, including the charming and ancient Mr Twentyman who lived, modestly, in a room on the ground floor and who loved to tell anyone prepared to listen the story of how his mother, when she was but a slip of a girl, had danced with a young Ned Kelly. He told this tale many times – as you would.

'Work began on the kitchen immediately; Georges designed and ordered square, rectangular and a few round wooden tables and selected some comfortable bistro chairs. I painted a very bold sign for outside and then hung some of my paintings on the walls to warm up the room. We found a very good French chef, gave thought to the sort of food we wanted to serve and, very soon, we opened Tolarno French Bistro,' remembers Mirka.

Like Café Balzac before it, the bistro was an overnight sensation; it was unlike anything that Fitzroy Street, or any other street in Melbourne for that matter, had ever seen. It had much in common with Balzac, notably the food, but because it was in St Kilda rather than in East Melbourne it had a rawness that came purely from the bistro's location, and that aspect was emphasised by the Moras as they began to understand its influence.

'So many people had told Georges that he was mad, and that he should not even think of opening a restaurant in St Kilda

⊛ Georges at the entrance to Tolarno, 1965
⊜ Mirka as many remember her, 1954.
⊙ Iain Hewitson and Mirka at Tolarno, early 1990s, Fitzroy Street, circa 1960

because it was a terrible place. Which it probably was in 1964. But, of course, it took about two minutes for Tolarno French Bistro to become the toast of Melbourne,' says Mirka.

There can be little doubt, in fact, that some of the seamier aspects of St Kilda – the real possibility of a thrilling criminal encounter or, at the very least, of seeing prostitutes and their minders and a colourful range of street thugs going about their nefarious business – became part of the attraction, just as the rawness of Harlem had attracted mid-town New Yorkers to fashionable clubs in that exotic quarter of Manhattan from the 1920s.

Tolarno French Bistro – which offered food that was simple enough, but dazzlingly progressive for the day – seemed to appeal to everyone. The very best of authentically bohemian and genuinely intellectual Melbourne rolled along – the writers, the painters, the musicians and the more imaginative of the academics. But the brilliance of the food, the ready availability of acceptable wine and the opportunity to rub shoulders with both the moderately famous and the creatively unwashed also attracted the smart set and even visiting members of the squattocracy from the Western District.

It appealed, indeed, to farmers, fairies and fabulists. As well as to perfectly ordinary lovers of reasonably priced, reliable French food of some distinction, a rare commodity in the 1960s, served in a setting that left you feeling as though you had somehow been transported to a table in an altogether livelier corner of the world. Which, in a sense, you had.

There were other attractions, of course: loud, thirsty painters, friends and acquaintances of both Georges and Mirka, would often dine at Tolarno. They were seldom required to pay but often behaved – or misbehaved – as though they owned the place. And generally, they were tolerated.

Once, famously, a food fight ensued between a table of painters, one or two of whom were later to become distinguished, and a larger table of graziers and their straitlaced wives and a couple of urban socialites, all of them wealthy. It ended

THE MORA YEARS

badly, and with Mirka, on behalf of her husband who was away at the time, gallantly taking responsibility for what turned out to be some monumental dry-cleaning bills; at least one of them involving the removal of intense black coffee from an expensive fur collar.

Now, the willingness of Georges to take responsibility for such matters as dry-cleaning bills, and to cover any other perceived deficiency with complimentary champagne, was in the nature of the man. But in Mirka's case, her anxiousness to absorb dry-cleaning costs may have had more to do with the fact that she was often responsible for the famed Tolarno food fights.

Mirka ensured, on quiet nights at the bistro – often aided and abetted by the Moras' old chum Charles Blackman, the painter – that things did not stay quiet for long. She had become expert at using a long spoon to propel a blob of chocolate mousse or a dollop of ripe camembert across the room, often with uncanny accuracy, and then ducking for cover. Her victims seldom suspected her, but enthusiastically responded to the challenge by firing some of their own food across the restaurant and embroiling fellow diners in vigorous exchanges.

'She loved to do it,' says William, 'and she usually got away with it. But while her aim was usually quite deadly, I remember one of her blobs of chocolate mousse hitting the ceiling and staying there.' It was up there for ages, he remembers – drying into a dark, guilty crust.

Also, it should be remembered, the enchanting Mirka was a significant drawcard. She could be relied upon, most evenings, to hold court in Tolarno or, at the very least, to be on duty – perhaps behind the small reception desk just inside the entrance where the cash register was to be found, and on which reclined her two formidable cats, only one of which displayed an enormous erection. Or so Mirka claims. Enormous for a cat, anyway.

On most nights, the Mora family, often with a fascinating guest or two, would occupy a table just inside the restaurant. Among the very few rules that Georges imposed upon his family was the dinner arrangement: all family members would gather, every night, on the dot of 7 pm, to dine together. As many as eight people, five of them Moras, would squeeze around a small, round table – spilling over to tables in front of the banquette only if absolutely necessary. Family gatherings and communications, perhaps one of the few remaining indicators of their Jewish origins, mattered to the Moras, and especially to Georges.

Georges and Mirka Mora, with the oldest of their sons – Paris-born Philippe, now an independent Hollywood-based film director – in tow, had arrived in Melbourne in 1951 with no intention of either owning or running restaurants. But the problem was this, as Georges later told an interviewer: it was impossible to find either a drinkable cup of coffee or an edible mayonnaise in Australia at the start of the 1950s. The coffee, he pointed out quite correctly, was unspeakable, and the mayonnaise, incomprehensibly to the urbane Georges, was sweet (and traditionally made, in those days, by shaking together, for three minutes

↪ Mirka, Georges and a fellow gourmet in the dining room at Tolarno

And when, after a time, they outgrew it, or it outgrew Exhibition Street, they opened Café Balzac in East Melbourne, an even wilder success which Georges sold, in the early 1960s, before going in search of all-purpose Mora family accommodation. Game on...

The neighbourhood, the food, the ambience, the sheer daring of it all – these were the things that helped to make Tolarno French Bistro in St Kilda what it quickly became. But it was the day on which Mirka Mora opened a couple of tins of Dulux and began to do what painters inevitably do when confronted with bare walls that the place began to develop into something more magical than even Georges had foreseen. Mirka's embellishments turned a conventional, modestly proportioned, low-ceilinged and generally undistinguished dining room into a living, breathing work of art and a veritable shrine to Melbourne's developing bohemianism and the awakenings of a city's taste for the more disreputable and less pretentious elements of the good life. What Mirka did was instinctive and, for her, partly therapeutic. But for Tolarno French Bistro, and for Melbourne diners, the result was revelatory.

in a jam jar with a screw-cap: vinegar, lemon juice, melted butter, an egg yolk or two, dry mustard, salt, cayenne and a generous amount of sweetened condensed milk).

'I had no prior experience in the restaurant trade,' Georges explained. 'But food is a pretty obvious occupation for a Frenchman. I had been eating out all of my life and I knew how good food should taste.'

To prove the point, Georges and Mirka had opened the Mirka Café in Exhibition Street in the first half of the 1950s. It was an instant success, especially with the art and literary set and the theatre crowds. It was extravagantly decorated with edgy contemporary art, and impromptu exhibitions were often staged. Through the café, also, both Georges and Mirka experienced at least some of the difficulties of operating such a business in Melbourne.

First, and rather tentatively, Mirka began to paint the wall nearest to the kitchen and surrounding the access doors. Her naïve, and yet strangely sophisticated images – of angels, geese, serpents, flowers and other fantastical creations – sprawled across that first section of wall, and from there gathered momentum and travelled around the room, eventually embellishing even the window glass with echoes of the deep green foliage of the grand she-oaks that lined the footpath. Forty years on, it is still possible to detect her growing confidence

and fluency and her increasing enthusiasm for her endeavours simply by running your eye around the walls in the order in which she painted them: her creations soon ceased simply to decorate the room and the bistro, and began to define it.

There is another exotic aspect to Mirka's wonderful windows, however, which William Mora remembers well.

'I can remember a drunken evening when Mirka and Charles [Blackman] began to paint the windows. It was one of those nights when Mirka would persuade her friends to stay on after dinner, turn out most of the lights in the bistro, and have an outrageous party. Outrageous but fabulous, of course,' he says.

'They would often take their clothes off and one night, I remember Mirka getting lots of sheets from the hotel's supply and handing them around. Everyone at the party took off their clothes and dressed in sheets, and it was mad. Mirka would often sweep a handful of room keys from their hooks in the hallway and hand them out, insisting that partygoers stay the night.

'Philippe and I loved those nights. We would often hide under a table and watch the most extraordinary acts of debauchery involving drunken adults. We were, I suppose, in our early teens at the time. It was great fun. And I have no doubt that the decision to paint the windows was partly to do with making the bistro a bit more private, and screening what was going on inside from anybody walking down Fitzroy Street. Some nights, the things they might have seen going on inside would have frightened the life out of passers-by.'

The essential appeal of Tolarno French

Bistro was, nevertheless, in the food on offer, initially produced by founding French chef Alain Guerin according to Georges' specifications. Alain trotted out all the usual bistro suspects that had starred at Café Balzac, with meals often opening with generous servings from an hors d'oeuvres selection. Onion soup was served, as were snails in garlic butter and oysters with a revolutionary – for the time – shallot vinaigrette. Traditional ragouts were popular and chocolate mousse was, one way or another, inescapable. Bread was broken by diners on the bare wooden tables without the use of side plates, and spread with unsalted butter. Cheeses were French, ripe and extravagantly flavoured by the standards of the day, and champagne and table wines flowed.

It was some years later, however, that mussels, offered as seductive moules marinière, were added to the menu when regular supplies of small, black, local examples were accessed first from Beaumaris and, later, from Flinders. To draw attention to the addition of this delicacy to the bill of fare, Georges had one of his few not entirely sound ideas: he posted raw mussels, one per envelope, to his regulars and to one or two worthies he hoped might become regulars, singing the praises of the delectable molluscs. Sadly, some were sent to business addresses where they languished aromatically over a weekend, while others were smashed in transit, and still others that had been incorrectly addressed were returned, in advanced stages of decomposition, to Tolarno. Despite this inauspicious beginning, local mussels quickly became a drawcard for the bistro, and moules marinière remained on top of the menu favourites for years to come.

Years later, Georges used the posted mussels stunt to promote another special occasion – his presentation of the restaurant's Grand Order of the Mussel. But he had learned something from his initial misadventure: this time, he posted out only mussel shells, attached to smart invitations. And on the night, the Grand Order went to none other than John Rossiter: a bon vivant, a state pollie of renown and, at the time, the father-in-law of Andrew Peacock who was married to his dazzling daughter, Susan – later to become Susan Sangster and, in time, Lady Renouf.

And so it was, more or less, that the Tolarno French Bistro legend was born – fathered by a stylish visionary who had developed into an inventive restaurateur after correctly assessing the urgent needs of a maturing society and making an inspired acquisition to accommodate the rather irregular needs of his extraordinary family. Georges had then seen his acquisition brought to life, spontaneously, by a gifted, other-worldly painter who just happened, also, to be a woman of great beauty, a creature of infinite mischief, and his wife.

⊕ Mirka in St Kilda, 1984

Champignons et Oignons à la Grecque
Salade de Céleri-Rave
Huîtres et Saucisses
Anchovy & Cheese Straws
Polenta Chips
Potted Smoked Salmon
Crumbed Mushrooms
La Terrine de Queue de Boeuf
Terrine de Langue, Porc et Épinards
Pâté de Foie Maison
Rillettes de Porc
Terrine du Chef
Garlic Bread
Pain Complet
Pissaladière
Dill & Cottage Cheese Bread

HORS D'OEUVRES,
Charcuterie & Breads

'What do you need to cook? You need the will. You need the desire. You need the determination to go on – even after you've scorched the first batch of stew, burned the sauce, mutilated the fish fillet and lopped off a hunk of fingertip.'

Anthony Bourdain
Les Halles Cookbook, 2004

Champignons et Oignons à la Grecque
(Mushrooms & Onions Poached in a Greek Broth)

425 ml water 75 ml olive oil juice of 1 large lemon ½ tsp sea salt 12 whole black peppercorns 12 whole fennel seeds 6 whole coriander seeds 6 sprigs fresh parsley ¼ red onion, finely chopped 1 celery stalk, finely diced	Bring to the boil.
12–18 baby (pickling) onions, peeled 450 gm button mushrooms, wiped with a damp cloth	Add onions to liquid and simmer for 10 minutes. Then add mushrooms and simmer for another 10 minutes. Remove vegetables and boil liquid to reduce by one-third. Strain over vegetables and chill. Serve with bread. Serves 6–8

Salade de Céleri-rave
(Celery Root with a Piquant Mayonnaise)

½ cup Homemade Mayonnaise (page 256) 1 heaped tsp Dijon mustard 1 garlic clove, crushed 2 anchovy fillets, mashed 1 tbsp drained & chopped capers 1 tbsp chopped fresh parsley	Mix together, adding a little more mayo to taste, if necessary.
2 celeriac, peeled & coarsely grated fresh lemon juice	Mix in along with lemon juice to taste. Serves 4

TOLARNO
FRENCH BISTRO

42 FITZROY STREET, ST KILDA, VICTORIA.
Proprietor: GEORGES MORA
TELE. 940521 (3 LINES)

APERITIFS

Moules Mariniere	1.75
French Onion Soup	70¢
Soup du Jour	60¢
Egg - Mayonnaise	65¢
Egg - Anchovis	65¢
Salami au Beurre	60¢
Sardines au Beurre	60¢
Oysters Natural - doz.	1.85
½ doz.	1.10
Canadian Smoked Salmon	1.95
Champignons a la Grecque	.95¢
Pate du Chef	.95¢
Hors d'oeuvres Varies	1.75
Escargots de Bourgogne - doz.	2.25
½ doz.	1.35
Cuisses de Grenouille (Frogs Legs)	2.30
Crevettes (Prawns) Frites, Sce Tartare	1.80 (Dinner 2.30)
Les Omelettes Varies	1.60

HOUSE WINE
Pichet 90¢

FISH

Filet de Whiting, Cecilia or Louisianna or Meuniere	2.50
Flounder Grenobloise, Flounder Espagnole	2.10
Truite Aux Amandes (Trout with Almonds)	2.20
Lobster Parisienne	3.20
Coquille St. Jacques	1.50 (Dinner 2.30)

Coonawarra Estate
Lindeman 45
Penfolds Kalimna
Saltram
McLaren Vale
Pokolbin
Seaview
St. Thomas
Oven Valley
Glenloth
McWilliams
Mount Pleasant
Hamilton

GRILLS

Steak au Poivre (Chef's Speciality)	2.90
Steak Grille Me d'Hotel	2.50
Filet Mignon, Me d'Hotel or Sce. Perigueux	2.90
Noisette de Boeuf Tyrolienne	2.50
Entrecote, Sce.	2.60
Steak Tartar Tolarno	2.80

POULTRY

Roast Chicken, Salade	2.30
Chicken Sauté - Provencale	2.30
Champignons Sautes	.80¢

SPECIALS TODAY

Great Western Brut
Romalo
Minchinbury Brut

French Wines

Spirits

CHEESE

Camembert - Danish Blue - Port Salut - St. Paulin	70¢

SWEETS

Creme Caramel	65¢
Tartuffo - Cassata	60¢
Mousse Aux Marrons	80¢
Mousse au Chocolat	80¢
Fresh Strawberries and Cream (In Season)	85¢

Cafe Filtre - 25¢

Huîtres et Saucisses
(Freshly Shucked Oysters with Spicy Sausages)

12 small spicy sausages (I like Merguez)	Preheat ridged grill or BBQ. Put sausages in just simmering water and cook until firmish when squeezed. Then grill or barbecue until well coloured.
4 dozen oysters, unopened but scrubbed	For this you need an oyster knife. Fold a clean tea towel a few times and put in your left hand. Put oyster on towel, hinge side out, and grab it firmly. Place hand on bench and push tip of knife into hinge. Work back and forth sideways until hinge gives. Then slide knife along top, releasing oyster. Lift off top shell, carefully keeping brine intact. Wet a finger and carefully brush around edge of shell and oyster to remove any shell fragments.
rock salt	Serve oysters on a bed of rock salt with sausages alongside.

Serves 4

'A traditional fisherman's snack, the principle of this dish is very simple – first of all an oyster, then a bite of sausage and to wash it down a slurp of crisp, dry white. And also don't forget another Tolarno favourite – Bloody Mary Oyster Shooters – just put an oyster in a shooter glass and top with Bloody Mary mix.'

Anchovy & Cheese Straws

4 sheets frozen puff pastry 15–18 anchovies	Preheat oven to 200°C. Place 2 pastry sheets on bench and arrange anchovies lengthways in 3 lines on top.
½ cup grated tasty cheese	Top each line with grated cheese.
1 egg ½ cup milk olive oil spray	Beat together and brush between the anchovy and cheese lines. Place 2 remaining sheets of pastry on top and press down firmly between lines. Then cut pastry carefully crossways into 2–3 cm–wide straws. Put on a lightly oiled baking tray, brush with eggwash and cook in oven until golden and risen (about 8 minutes). Serves 8–12

'A delicious starter or accompaniment to a soup.'

Polenta Chips

a little chicken stock 2 garlic cloves, peeled	In a small pot cook gently until tender. Set aside.
250 gm polenta 2 cups cold water	Combine polenta with water in a bowl.
2 cups cold water sea salt	In a large heavy bottomed pot, bring lightly salted water to the boil. Add polenta and cook, over moderate heat, for 5 minutes, stirring continually. Turn heat down to low and continue to cook polenta for about 30 minutes, stirring frequently, until it comes away from the sides of pot.
100 gm freshly grated parmesan olive oil spray	Chop garlic and mix into polenta with parmesan. Turn out into an oiled tray to about 1.5 cm thick. Smooth out to an even thickness, cover and refrigerate overnight.
plain flour 2 eggs 1 cup milk 2–3 cups breadcrumbs	The next day cut into 1.5 x 8 cm lengths. Put flour in one bowl, beaten eggs and milk in another, and crumbs in a third. Dip polenta into flour, then into eggwash and firmly into crumbs.
6 cups vegetable oil Dijon Mustard Aïoli (page 256)	Heat oil in a wok or deep-fryer to about 180°C and, without overcrowding, fry polenta chips until golden brown. Drain well on kitchen paper towels and serve with aïoli on the side.

Serves 4—6

'Along with the crumbed mushrooms, this was one of our most popular starters.'

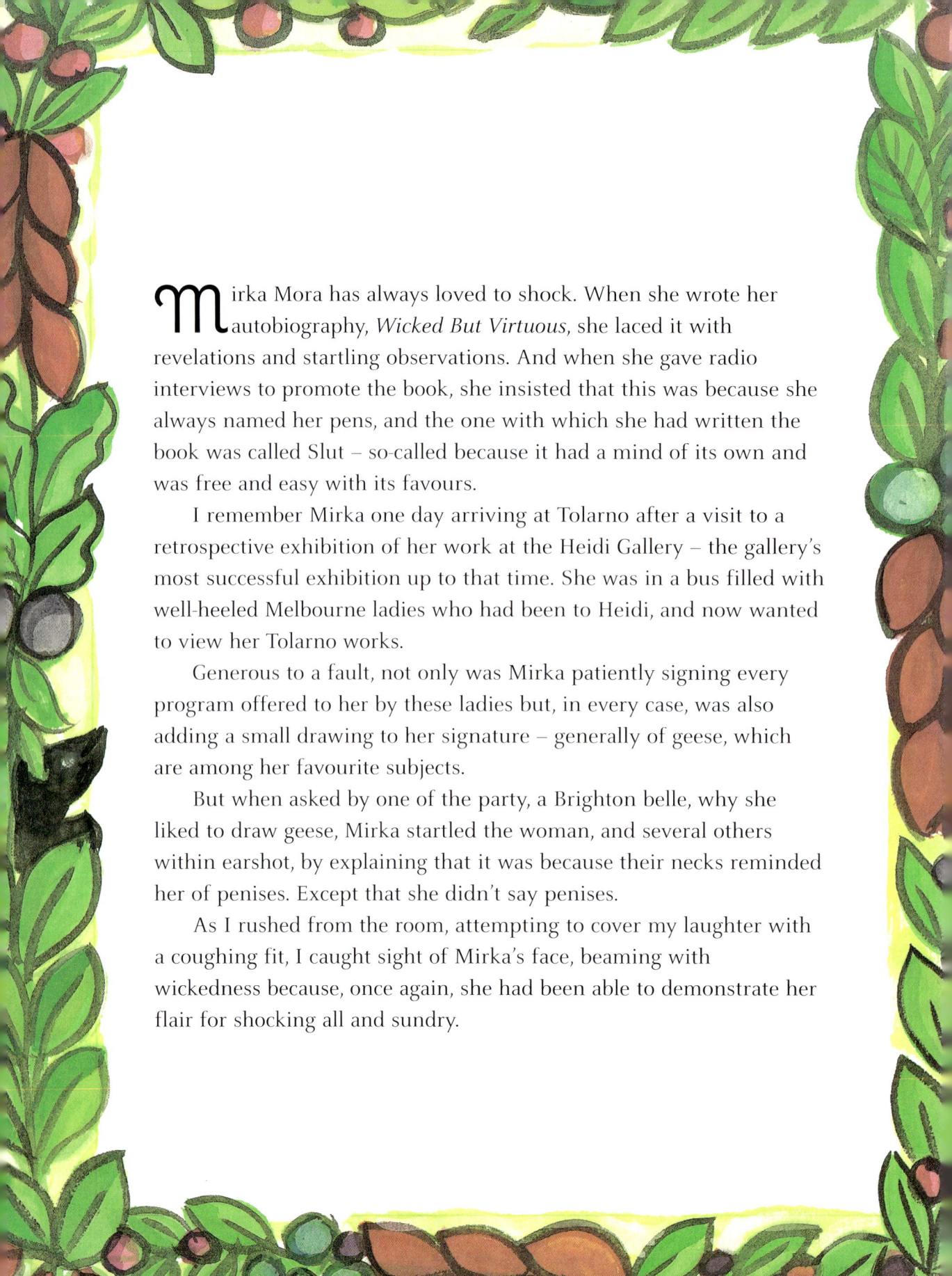

Mirka Mora has always loved to shock. When she wrote her autobiography, *Wicked But Virtuous*, she laced it with revelations and startling observations. And when she gave radio interviews to promote the book, she insisted that this was because she always named her pens, and the one with which she had written the book was called Slut – so-called because it had a mind of its own and was free and easy with its favours.

I remember Mirka one day arriving at Tolarno after a visit to a retrospective exhibition of her work at the Heidi Gallery – the gallery's most successful exhibition up to that time. She was in a bus filled with well-heeled Melbourne ladies who had been to Heidi, and now wanted to view her Tolarno works.

Generous to a fault, not only was Mirka patiently signing every program offered to her by these ladies but, in every case, was also adding a small drawing to her signature – generally of geese, which are among her favourite subjects.

But when asked by one of the party, a Brighton belle, why she liked to draw geese, Mirka startled the woman, and several others within earshot, by explaining that it was because their necks reminded her of penises. Except that she didn't say penises.

As I rushed from the room, attempting to cover my laughter with a coughing fit, I caught sight of Mirka's face, beaming with wickedness because, once again, she had been able to demonstrate her flair for shocking all and sundry.

Potted Smoked Salmon

200 gm unsalted butter	To clarify the butter, melt, gently, in a small pot. Skim impurities off top. Then pour off clear butter, leaving any milky residue behind.
300 gm smoked salmon, diced juice of 1 lemon 1 heaped tbsp snipped fresh chives a few splashes of Tabasco sea salt & freshly ground pepper	Mix together and put into 4 dariole moulds or one large soufflé dish. Pour clarified butter over top and refrigerate overnight.
sour cream salmon caviar sliced sourdough bread, toasted	Turn out of moulds, place a dollop of sour cream and some salmon caviar on top, and serve with toasted sourdough alongside.

Serves 4

Crumbed Mushrooms

6 cups vegetable oil	Heat in a fryer or wok to 190°C.
plain flour 2 eggs 1 cup milk 2–3 cups breadcrumbs 40 firm baby button mushrooms, wiped with a damp cloth	Put flour in one bowl, whisked eggs and milk in another and breadcrumbs in a third. Then crumb mushrooms by dipping into flour first, then into eggwash and firmly into crumbs.
Tartare Sauce (page 256)	Fry in two or three lots until golden. Drain well on kitchen paper towels and serve with tartare on the side.

Serves 4

'I know this has featured in another book, but how could I leave out Tolarno's all time favourite starter – I think we most probably sold about 10 million of the blessed things.'

La Terrine de Queue de Boeuf
(Jellied Oxtail Terrine)

1.5 kilos oxtail, cut into 10 cm pieces

1 tbsp sea or rock salt
6 carrots, coarsely chopped
2 leeks, white part only, cleaned & chopped
2 celery stalks, coarsely chopped
1 onion, coarsely chopped
2 garlic cloves, crushed
1 bouquet garni (12 fresh parsley stems, 8 peppercorns, ¼ tsp fresh thyme leaves, ¼ tsp fennel seeds & 1 bay leaf tied in a double thickness of cheesecloth)

Two days before you intend using the terrine, tie the oxtail in a large bundle with string. Place in a large heavy-bottomed pot, cover with cold water and bring to simmer for 20 minutes, skimming regularly. Move pot halfway off heat and simmer for another 20 minutes, continuing to skim off any foam or impurities carefully. Add rest of ingredients and simmer for 3–4 hours until meat is falling off the bone, skimming as necessary. Cool and refrigerate overnight. The next day, remove fat from top. Remove oxtail and shred meat with a fork, discarding fat. Then put jelly over heat until just liquid and strain.

---

12 baby carrots, peeled & sliced into rounds
2 tbsp drained & chopped capers
sea salt & freshly ground pepper

Cook carrots until tender in boiling water (overcook slightly). Add to oxtail along with capers and pack into terrine moulds. Season liquid generously and pour over to just cover. Cover and refrigerate for at least a day.

---

horseradish cream
cornichons (baby gherkins)
crusty bread

To serve, unmould, slice with an electric knife and serve with horseradish cream, cornichons and plenty of bread.

Serves 12

'A very popular dish in the latter years at Tolarno, the recipe comes from "Bistro Cooking" by Patricia Wells. And while it does take a little bit of forward planning, the end result is so delicious it is well worth the effort.'

Terrine de Langue, Porc et Épinards
(Tongue, Pork & Spinach Terrine)

480 gm lean pork mince
240 gm diced, cooked ox tongue
120 gm diced pork back fat
4 eggs
a good pinch of nutmeg
2 cups blanched, well-drained spinach, chopped
150 ml thickened cream
150 gm cleaned chicken livers, cubed
1 tbsp sea salt
2 tbsp gelatine, softened in cold water
15 sprigs fresh rosemary & 3 tbsp fresh herbs, chopped together

Preheat oven to 220°C.
Mix together well.

finely sliced pork fat or rindless bacon
sliced sourdough bread, toasted
cornichons (baby gherkins)

Line terrine mould with pork fat or bacon (allowing slices to overhang so that they can be folded over the filling). Fill with mixture, cover with fat and then with foil. Cook in oven for 1 hour. Turn down to 180°C and cook for another 45 minutes. Then top with a board and heavy cans or weights and, when cold, refrigerate at least overnight. Put hot towels around terrine to help remove, slice thickly and serve with toasted sourdough and cornichons.

Severs 12

Pâté de Foie Maison
(House Liver Pâté)

700 gm cleaned duck or chicken livers sea salt	Blanch livers in salted water for a minute or so. Then drain and coarsely chop.
150 gm unsalted butter 200 gm rindless bacon, diced	Melt butter and gently sauté bacon until tender. Turn up heat, add livers and toss for a few minutes.
3 tbsp port	Add and bubble briefly.
4 tbsp thickened cream sea salt & freshly ground pepper	Add and whiz up in a blender until smooth. Push through a fine sieve and put into 8 dariole moulds or soufflé dishes.
clarified butter (page 53) sliced sourdough bread, toasted	When cool, top with a layer of clarified butter and refrigerate. Serve with toast.

Serves 8

'I think every bistro in Australia (including Tolarno) would have featured Pâté Maison in one form or other on their menus throughout the sixties and seventies.'

Rillettes de Porc
(Slow-cooked Shredded Pork Pâté in its own fat)

1 kilo rindless pork belly 250 gm pork back fat	Preheat oven to 140°C. Cube and put in a heavy-bottomed pot.
1 tsp allspice 6 garlic cloves, chopped a good pinch of nutmeg 4 bay leaves sea salt & freshly ground pepper 2 tsp paprika 150 ml dry sherry 1 tsp crushed fennel seeds	Add, combine and tightly cover with foil and a lid. Cook in oven for 4 hours and then strain, reserving all the juices.
melted duck fat	When cool enough to handle (but not cold), shred meat with your fingers and then mix back into juices. Put into ramekins, press down to level out and top with a layer of duck fat. Refrigerate until set.
cornichons (baby gherkins) sliced sourdough bread, toasted	Serve alongside. Serves 10

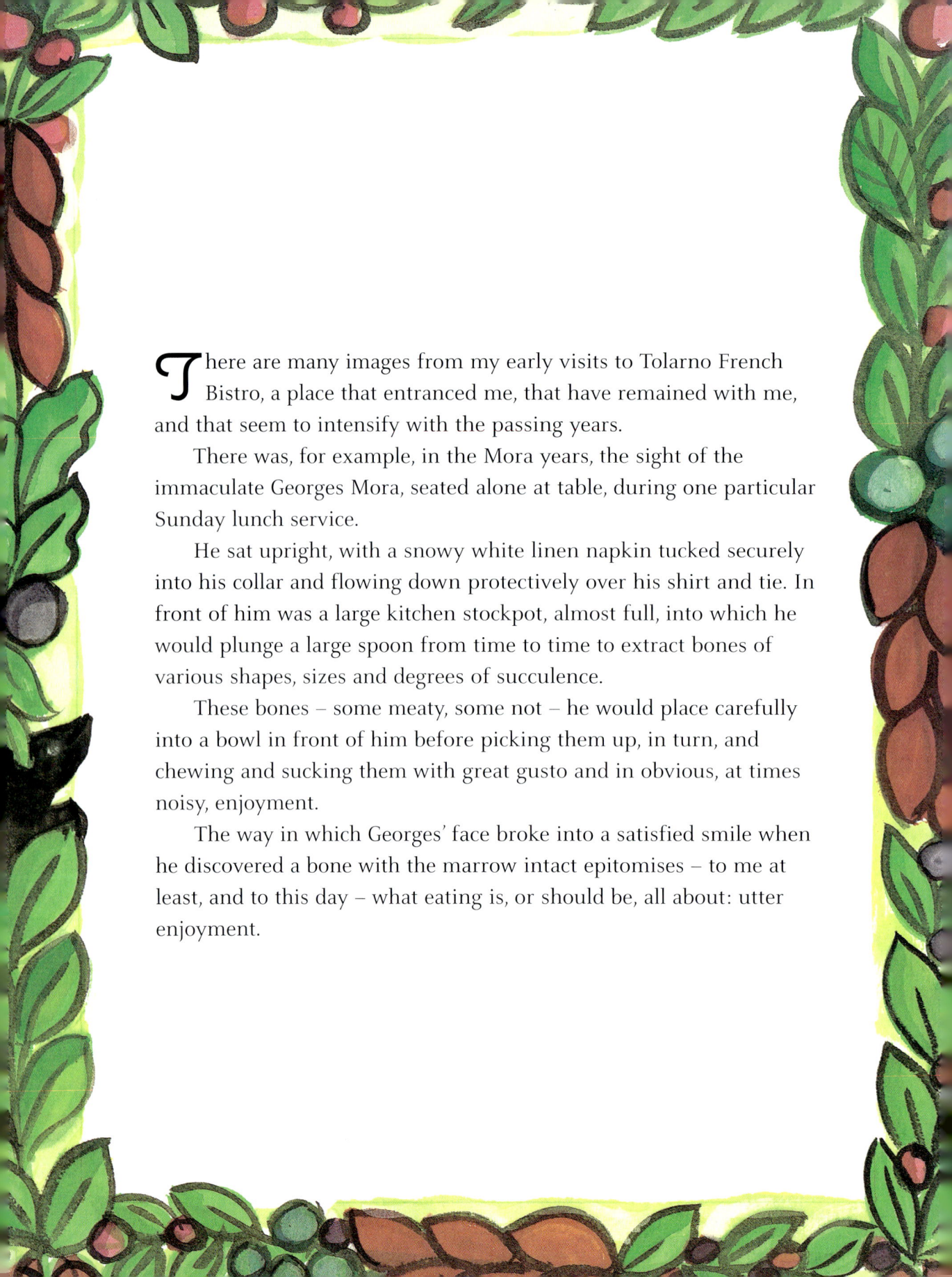

There are many images from my early visits to Tolarno French Bistro, a place that entranced me, that have remained with me, and that seem to intensify with the passing years.

There was, for example, in the Mora years, the sight of the immaculate Georges Mora, seated alone at table, during one particular Sunday lunch service.

He sat upright, with a snowy white linen napkin tucked securely into his collar and flowing down protectively over his shirt and tie. In front of him was a large kitchen stockpot, almost full, into which he would plunge a large spoon from time to time to extract bones of various shapes, sizes and degrees of succulence.

These bones – some meaty, some not – he would place carefully into a bowl in front of him before picking them up, in turn, and chewing and sucking them with great gusto and in obvious, at times noisy, enjoyment.

The way in which Georges' face broke into a satisfied smile when he discovered a bone with the marrow intact epitomises – to me at least, and to this day – what eating is, or should be, all about: utter enjoyment.

Terrine du Chef
(The Chef's Pork, Veal & Liver Terrine)

olive oil 1 onion, chopped 2 garlic cloves, crushed	Preheat oven to 180°C. Heat oil in a heavy-bottomed pan and sauté until tender.
450 gm cleaned duck or chicken livers, cubed	Add and toss until well sealed. Remove to a bowl.
150 ml port	Add to pan and reduce by half. Scrape into a bowl.
350 gm lean pork, minced 350 gm lean veal, minced 225 gm pork back fat, minced 2 eggs, lightly beaten 1 ½ tsp sea salt a pinch of freshly ground pepper 2 good pinches allspice	Add and beat vigorously by hand with a wooden spoon. Sauté a small spoonful to check seasoning.
finely sliced pork back fat or rindless bacon rashers	Line a terrine mould with pork fat or bacon, allowing it to overhang sides. Fill with mixture and fold overhanging fat over top. Cover with foil and put in a deep pan with boiling water two-thirds up the side. Cook in oven for about 1 ½ hours until terrine has shrunk a little from sides and liquid is clear. Remove, pour off water and when cool top terrine with board and some weights or heavy cans and refrigerate overnight.
cornichons (baby gherkins) sliced sourdough bread, toasted	To serve, cut in thick slices and serve with cornichons and toasted sourdough.

Serves 12

Garlic Bread

100 gm soft unsalted butter
3 garlic cloves, crushed
2 tbsp chopped fresh parsley
juice of ½ lemon

Preheat oven to 220°C.
Combine with your hands, until well mixed.

1 baguette

Cut through centre lengthways. Generously spread both sides with garlic butter. Reform, place on baking tray and cook in oven until butter has melted right through and bread is crusty.

Serves 4–6

'Nothing like the soggy version served in most bistros during the seventies. I still remember the Tolarno customer who always had a bowl of soup ($4.50) and three serves of garlic bread (free). I felt I should have just given him $5 and told him to go away.'

Pain Complet
(Wholemeal Bread)

3 ¾ cups stone-ground wholemeal flour	Place flour in a bowl and put in warm oven (gas with pilot light on only, electric on as low as it will go).
1 ½ tbsp fresh yeast 1 cup warm water 2 tbsp molasses 1 tbsp sea salt	Dissolve yeast in water and then whisk in molasses and salt. Add to flour.
1 cup warm water olive oil spray	Mix in up to one cup water (mixture should be firm but not too dry). Put in a lightly oiled bread tin, cover and allow to rise by one-third in a warm spot.
	Preheat oven to 220°C. Cook in oven for 50 minutes. To check that it is ready, turn out and rap bottom with your knuckles – it should sound hollow. Then leave out of tin in turned-off oven for 10 minutes. Makes 1–2 loaves

'This makes great toast and, because it only needs one rising, is a very simple bread to whip up.'

Pissaladière
(A Provençal Pizza)

1 cup lukewarm water 1 tbsp dry yeast 1 cup strong bread flour a pinch of sugar	Combine in a bowl. Stir well and leave until foaming (5 or so minutes).
1 tsp sea salt 1 ½ cups strong bread flour	Add salt to mixture and then add up to 1 ½ cups flour until mixture is no longer sticky. Knead on a floured bench with the palm of your hand until smooth and elastic. Put in a large bowl, cover with plastic wrap and leave, in a warm spot, for about 1 hour or until doubled in size. Then punch down to deflate the yeasts' gases and allow fermentation to begin again. Cover and leave until doubled in size. This can be done the day before and kept in a sealed container in the fridge.
olive oil 4 medium onions, sliced 2 garlic cloves, crushed 6 ripe, red tomatoes, cored & finely diced a few sprigs of fresh thyme sea salt & freshly ground pepper	When dough is ready, preheat oven to 230°C. Heat a little oil in a pan and sauté onions and garlic until tender. Then add tomatoes, thyme and seasoning and cook gently for 15–20 minutes.
olive oil spray 6 pieces roasted red capsicum, diced (page 68) 10 pitted black olives, sliced 6 olive-oil preserved artichoke hearts, chopped 10 anchovies, roughly chopped extra virgin olive oil	Roll out dough on a lightly floured bench. Then place in a lightly oiled baking tray or free form cake tin. Spread onion mixture over top. Then mix together capsicum, olives, artichokes and anchovies and scatter over the top. Sprinkle with extra virgin olive oil and cook in oven for about 20 minutes. To serve, cut into squares or triangles. Serves 8–10

Dill & Cottage Cheese Bread

15 gm fresh yeast 1 cup tepid water	Dissolve yeast in water. Prove for approximately 10 minutes, until foaming.
2 cups soft cottage cheese 2 tbsp sugar 1 onion, whizzed up in a processor 2 tbsp unsalted butter	Mix in a bowl, then add yeast mix.
1 cup chopped fresh dill 2 tsp sea salt ½ tsp baking soda 2 eggs, unbeaten	Add.
approximately 5 cups plain flour	Add enough flour to make a stiff dough, mixing thoroughly.
olive oil	Put in a bowl, cover and let rise in a warm spot until doubled in size. Knock down, knead lightly and put in oiled bread tins. Let rise again to top of tin.
	Preheat oven to 180°C. Cook in oven for 40–45 minutes or until golden brown and hollow when tapped on bottom. Makes 1–2 loaves

'One of my all time favourites.'

On a stifling summer night in St Kilda, the irrepressible Mirka Mora was standing outside the front door of Tolarno French Bistro – looking stunning, and wearing as little as possible, as she was inclined to do, to compensate for the heat. And as she stood there, a male friend stopped for a chat.

Now Mirka could hardly be described as either shy or retiring. But she was deeply offended when two police officers, who had been lurking around a corner, pounced, and threatened to arrest her for soliciting. Her friend, naturally, found it all hilarious. As did the police officers when she tried to convince them she was, in fact, the proprietor of the stylish establishment, at the front door of which she was standing.

Mercifully, Georges heard the commotion, wandered out, and managed to convince two of Melbourne's finest that Mirka was indeed his wife, the proprietor of Tolarno French Bistro, and to the best of his knowledge was by no means available on a hourly basis.

Whereupon the two diligent, but by now red-faced constables apologised, and went about their business.

Some debatable history

There is surprisingly little that we know, with absolute certainty, about the history of Tolarno – the building in which almost everything that unfolds in these pages took place. We know that the building was commissioned, completed and paid for to the tune of some £220 (excluding the cost of land, which was £50) by an almost certainly distinguished and clearly wealthy gentleman called John Stedeford in 1884. But beyond that, and a few planning details, we must allow speculation to be our guide, and approach the issue with a similar enthusiasm for embellishment and approximation (but not, I trust, misdirection) to that expressed and often practised by the magnificent and contrary Mirka Mora.

My suspicions – for reasons, based on the boldest of assumptions, that I shall outline later – are that Mr Stedeford was an English immigrant, possibly from North Devon. For such a man, the decision to build an elegant Victorian mansion in the pleasing bayside resort of St Kilda – a stimulating train ride from Melbourne's Flinders Street station, on Victoria's first passenger rail service – was the equivalent of a British gentleman choosing to build an elegant home for his family in Brighton, say. Or Bath. The house Mr Stedeford commissioned and funded was of brick, had twelve rooms, and was set well back on its block at 42 Fitzroy Street, leaving sufficient room in front for a regulation croquet lawn on which mallets were wielded, balls collided noisily, fine shots were applauded politely and, between games, where tea – probably Darjeeling – was poured into bone china cups and taken with cucumber sandwiches. The house was of two floors with a fine Italianate balcony on the first and a matching, similarly arched and columned, portico on the ground.

But how, you may well ask, could I possibly have deduced – speculated might be a better word, on this occasion – that the good Mr Stedeford came from North Devon? Well …

Stedeford is an uncommon name. It no longer appears in any Australian capital city telephone directory. But once, it was a name that attracted, for Melbourne, world attention. It belonged to a popular singer called Marjorie Stedeford who was the first performer to sing the words of the hit song 'Body and Soul' which was written in 1930 by Edward Heyman, Robert Sour, Frank Eyton and John Green and, in time, drew great performances from jazz legends Billie Holiday, Ella Fitzgerald, Sarah Vaughan and, perhaps most famously, inspired a legendary solo from tenor saxophonist Coleman

Hawkins. But Marjorie Stedeford recorded it, too, and hers, for the English market in particular, was the first, definitive version. She had moved to London in 1935 and found herself at the centre of a popular music boom. Everything seemed to be going swimmingly for her until, at the height of her fame, war was declared, and Marjorie decided to return home. To Melbourne. Where she died, aged just 50, in 1959.

But Marjorie was not simply from Melbourne. She had been born, in 1909, in St Kilda. Her father was John Stedeford, a descendant of English Stedefords from North Devon, say the records of the day. And Marjorie was the youngest of three children. But ... is it possible? Could her John Stedeford be our mysterious Tolarno John? Or was her father the son of Tolarno John? Or is the name, and the St Kilda association, all just pure coincidence?

Well, perhaps it is. But it is the sort of coincidence that might, at the very least, inspire a painting from Mirka Mora. And the sort of coincidence that fits, to perfection, the magic that has long been a part of Tolarno. It is therefore a coincidence that deserves our serious consideration and around which we should all, at the very least, roll our tongues.

But whether or not the golden-voiced Marjorie was a direct descendant of Tolarno's John Stedeford, which is probable, she was certainly not born in Tolarno. Because for reasons unknown, Mr Stedeford sold his house (which may or may not have been called Tolarno at that point as we shall also discuss later) to a Mr James Fairchild (occupation: gentleman) only a couple of years after having taken up residence. Sadly, the youthful Mr Fairchild died in the year he purchased it – 1887 – and the house was acquired, advantageously, by a Mr Ross Macartney who is variously described in council documentation as a manufacturer, a

⊕ Tolarno facade, Fitzroy Street, St Kilda, circa 1960

⊕ Plans for alterations and renovations to Tolarno, 1927

merchant and, by 1891, manager of the Mutual Store in Flinders Street, Melbourne.

In 1893, an owner who was to make a lasting impression on the place, and the suburb, appeared. His name was Thomas Atherton; his occupation, also, was gentleman, of whom there seemed to be a goodly number in the parish in those days. He had bought the place at a knockdown price – certainly for less than it had cost John Stedeford to build – and he owned it until 1931, by which time it was worth, curiously, not a penny more.

Little is known of Mr Atherton: his importance, however, lies in the fact that, if we are to accept the evidence of council papers which first began to call the place Tolarno in 1899, the possibility arises of Mr Atherton being the man who named it. But was this really the case? Or was it a simply a matter of the name of a property being unimportant in council documents up to that point, as councils tend to deal purely in addresses and property owners?

After having walked a considerable distance in the shoes of Tolarno, I am inclined to think that it carried the name from the day John Stedeford commissioned it. But who can say for sure? According to council records, it became a rooming house in about 1910, with more dramatic additions in the 1940s and the disappearance of the croquet lawn. It also earns a passing mention by name in a historical book written about St Kilda. Which would certainly fit the theory that it was named by Mr Atherton in 1899, as council records suggest.

But wait. Because from far away, from a vast sheep station in a remote corner of New

⊙ Postcard of Fitzroy St, St Kilda, circa 1912

South Wales, comes a very different tale, a new theory. And to me at least, a far more poetic and seductive one ...

It was in 1855, some 29 years before John Stedeford reached into his deep pockets in St Kilda's Fitzroy Street, that William and Ross Reid, Scottish adventurers and pioneers, took possession of an abandoned frontage on the eastern side of the Darling River, 160 kilometres south-east of Broken Hill. They called the place Tolarno – a name that allegedly had its origins in the words 'to the Arno' or 'to l'Arno', referring to the Italian river on which Florence is built. And while this etymological theory confounds linguists and geographers alike, and sounds strangely improbable to the rest of us, it has been faithfully recorded in station records, and is accepted by many. Including, curiously, Mirka Mora – who may even have had a hand in its popularization, having outlined it in a letter to Tolarno Station in the early Mora years of Tolarno French Bistro.

The Reid brothers, an ingenious and visionary pair, achieved success not only beyond their wildest dreams, but success which is hard for us to comprehend, even today. The money they generated annually from their venture, which they cunningly expanded to a property of a million acres from which they shore an astonishing 300,000 sheep, soon ran into the equivalent of hundreds of millions of dollars in today's money.

The Reids not only ran sheep, but also operated a fleet of steamships on which they transported their wool, and the occasional passenger, down the Murray to Port Victor. And in 1884, the pride of their fleet was a

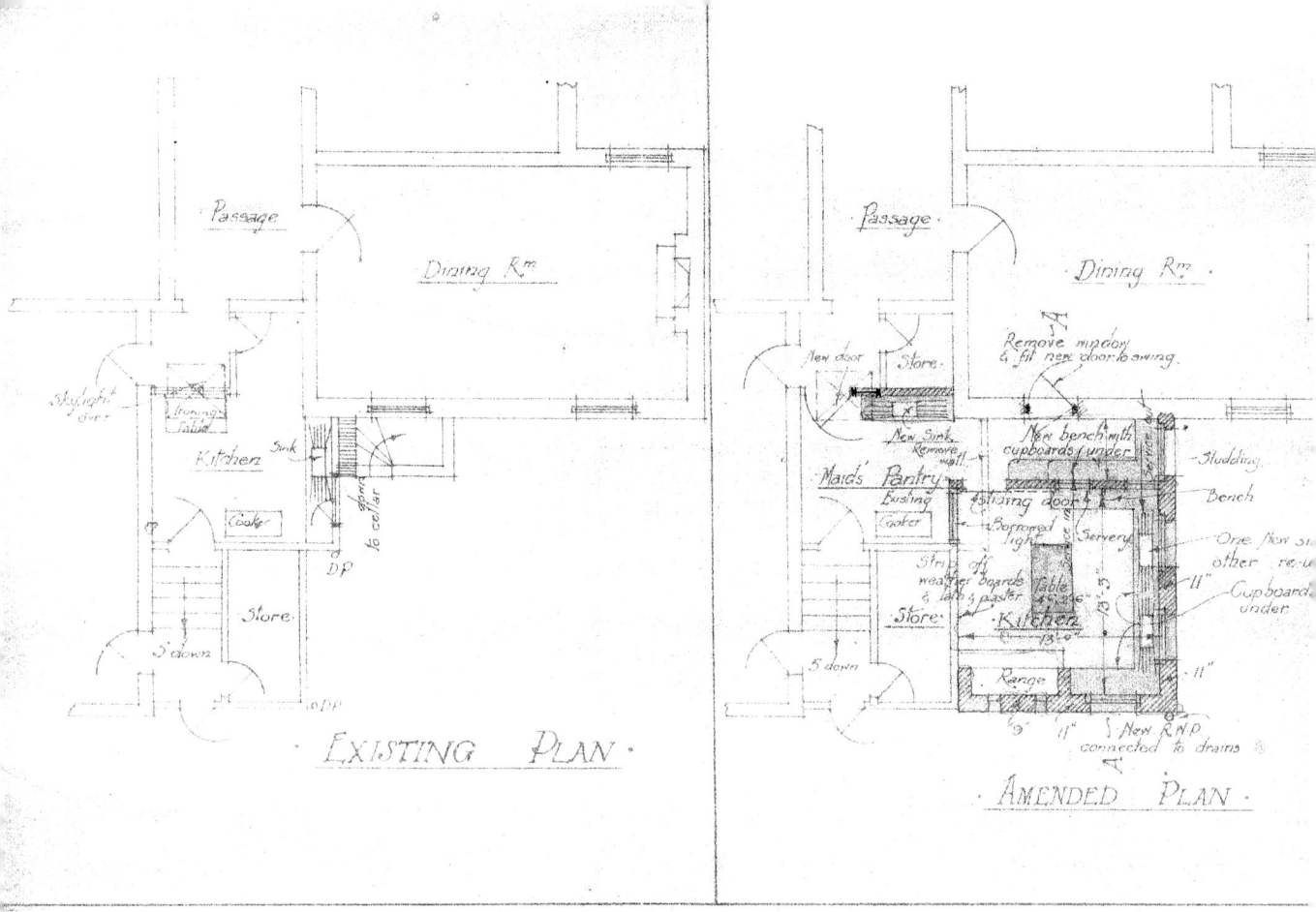

↑ Plans for alterations and renovations to Tolarno, 1927

gleaming new craft called, coincidentally, Tolarno. A painting of this handsome vessel now hangs over the fireplace in the historic Tolarno homestead, a place at which Burke and Wills famously rested on their fateful journey and still a working station in the hands of Robert and Linda McBride. Though now it is a mere 250,000-acre property running 10,000 sheep and 150 cattle – and still called Tolarno.

In early 1868 Ross Reid married Lucy Reynell whose family were the founders of the famous Reynella Winery which produced fine wines that, curiously, were later to find their way onto the wine lists of various Tolarno bistros. Now, whether a marriage into the wine trade increased the cashed-up Reid brothers' enthusiasm for the good life, who can say? But enthusiastic they certainly were, and their city of choice, to which they liked to repair from their remote empire, was Melbourne. The city also satisfied their passion for the turf: in the second half of the nineteenth century they twice entered horses in the Melbourne Cup and on both occasions their horses finished in second place.

They were well known, in those days, were the Reids of Tolarno. All of which gave the property added appeal, and its name added exposure. And my theory, therefore, as to how the name Tolarno came to be attached to a stylish St Kilda building is, quite simply, that John Stedeford was a man with time to digest the social pages and the gossip columns of the day. Success, it is often believed, breeds success. And one has only to consider the way in which the names of successful restaurants are recycled in other cities to understand the principle: Tolarno, whatever it may have meant, and whence it may have come, was a solid-gold name at the very moment when John Stedeford was making his grand investment – his contribution to carefree Melbourne society during its own Belle Époque. And all at a time when St Kilda, with its gentle ocean breezes, stately buildings and a suitable measure of separation from the noise and bustle and rough and tumble of Melbourne, was a fine place in the world to be – a more suitable place for a gentle game of garden croquet, a nice cup of tea, a glass or two of Reynella port or sherry and a chorus or two of 'Body and Soul', than most.

But was Tolarno, St Kilda, the Victorian residence of the fabulously wealthy Reids of Tolarno, New South Wales, as some glancing-blow historians suggest? I think not. There are no names anywhere in the records of building ownership that point to this. But does it really matter? Or could we, more profitably and in line with the philosophies of Mirka Mora and other free spirits who have emerged from St Kilda, turn our thoughts to the admirable 'Sonnet to St Kilda' which appeared in the pages of Melbourne Punch on 26 June 1856? I think so.

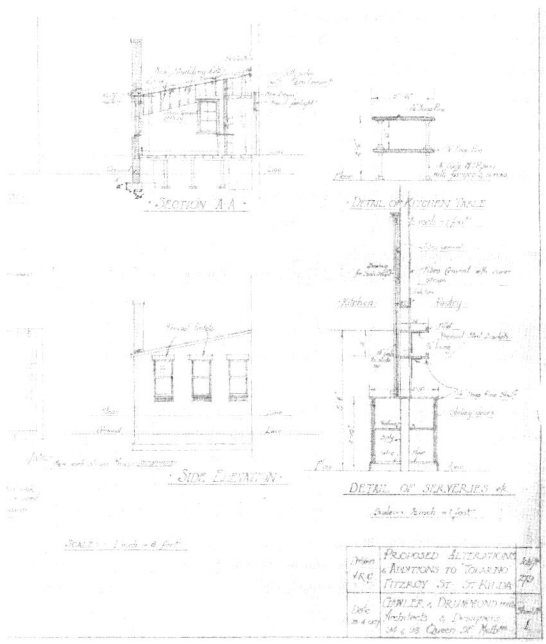

⬆ Plans for alterations and renovations to Tolarno, 1927

The poem goes like this:

How beautiful St Kilda do appear
The air just gives an appetite for vittles
Prime place to get an oyster and some beer,
And pass an afternoon a playing skittles,
Nice place to come and get a briny soak,
Which costs including towels, just a bob,
And when one's had a nobbler and a smoke,
What pleasant fancies fills a fellow's nob.
Here on the beach you see the ladies stroll,
Softly basking in the morning sun,
There's a black eyed beauty (bless her soul)
As agitates my bosom – she's the one,
The loveliest face inside the littlest bonnet,
To her I dedicate my humblest sonnet.
– Anon

Escargots à la Bourguignonne
Soufflé de Homard
Prawn Cocktail
Flamiche aux Poireaux
Artichauts Hollandaise
Asparagus with Double Peeled Broad beans, Olive Oil, Balsamic & Parmesan
Gratin de Macaroni et Mais
House Salted Fish Cakes with Dijon Mustard Aïoli
Slow-roasted Tomatoes on Sourdough with Feta
Poireaux Grillée et Sauce Gribiche
Zucchini Flowers Stuffed with a Scallop Mousseline
Soufflés à la Suissesse
Oeufs Sur le Plat 'Florentine'
Potato Blini with Smoked Salmon & Salmon Caviar
Ratatouille Niçoise et Oeufs Pochés
Crème Crecy
Garbure
Soupe au Pistou
Crème Vichyssoise Glacée
Snow Pea Soup with a Splash of Champagne
Soupe à l'Oignon Gratinée
Soupe Cultivateur

ENTREES
& Soups

'The Frenchman is an individualist. On its reverse side this may make him selfish and an egotist. But I am glad that France is full of his kind to keep French cooks up to snuff. His favourite bistro may have produced for him a thousand superb meals one after the other, but let the thousand and first be unsatisfactory and he rises in wrath to denounce incompetence.'

Waverley Root
The Food of France, 1958

Escargots à la Bourguignonne
(Snails in Garlic Butter)

48 canned snails with shells	Preheat oven to 200°C. Rinse under cold water and drain well.
½ red onion, finely chopped 1 cup dry white wine	Put in a pot with snails. Simmer very, very gently for 10 minutes. Drain.
1 anchovy, chopped ¼ cup chopped fresh Italian (flat leaf) parsley ½ tbsp sea salt 6 garlic cloves, crushed fresh ground pepper	To make Garlic Butter, throw in a processor and whiz up until smooth.
250 gm soft unsalted butter	Add little by little, blending between each addition. Then put a little of the butter mixture in bottom of each shell, top with snails and fill with more butter, pressing in. Cook in oven until bubbling and hot.
baguette	Serve with bread to mop up juices. Serves 10–12

'Another early Tolarno classic, which has seemingly gone out of fashion – maybe it deserves another 15 minutes of fame.'

Soufflé de Homard
(Lobster Soufflé)

melted butter plain flour	Preheat oven to 180°C. Butter and flour 6–8 largish soufflé dishes.
55 gm butter 55 gm plain flour	Melt butter in a heavy-bottomed pot, add flour and cook over moderate heat for a few minutes.
600 ml milk 350 gm cooked lobster, finely chopped 160 gm grated tasty cheese	Heat milk and add all at once, whisking vigorously. Stir until thickened. Add any 'mustard' from lobster, together with cheese. Cook to melt cheese.
sea salt & freshly ground pepper	Add lobster and season to taste. Cook gently for a couple of minutes.
8 egg yolks	Beat a little, then gradually mix into hot sauce.
10 egg whites	Beat to fairly stiff peaks, then fold into mixture little by little. Put in prepared soufflé dishes and wrap a collar of buttered foil around top. Cook for 15–20 minutes or until centre moves only slightly when gently shaken. Remove foil collar and serve immediately. Serves 6–8

'To make this dish even more special, serve the soufflés with the lobster sauce on page 114.'

Prawn Cocktail

½ cup Homemade Mayonnaise (page 256)
1–2 tbsp tomato ketchup
1 tsp cognac
2–3 shakes Tabasco
a squeeze of fresh lemon juice

Mix together, adding a little hot water if too thick.

---

2 dozen cooked medium-sized prawns

Peel and devein.

---

inner heart of 1 crisp, green iceberg lettuce
1 spring (green) onion, finely shredded

Toss together and place in glasses. Top with prawns and spoon sauce over.

---

4 lemon wedges
4 cooked medium-sized whole prawns, shell intact

Garnish with a lemon wedge and a prawn.

Serves 4

'It is a bit of a shame that the prawn cocktail has disappeared from our menus. It is no wonder – bad prawns and bad mayo do not a prawn cocktail make. Only ever use the best Australian prawns, make your own mayonnaise (trust me, it's simple) and, last but not least, use Heinz Tomato Ketchup – it doesn't work with the everyday tomato sauce.'

Flamiche aux Poireaux
(Leek & Cheese Tart)

2 cups plain flour, sifted ½ tsp sea salt 2 pinches sugar 2 tbsp vegetable shortening 115 gm cold unsalted butter, cut into cubes	Make shortcrust pastry by putting in a large bowl. Rub flour, shortening and butter together with your fingertips until mixture is like breadcrumbs.
1 tbsp baking powder 1 egg yolk about ⅓ cup water plain flour	Add baking powder and egg yolk, along with enough water to make a smooth, soft dough (should be pliable but not sticky). Sprinkle lightly with flour, roll into a ball and put in freezer for 1 hour.
500 gm leeks, washed well & cut into rounds 1/2 cup water a good dollop of butter	Simmer in a heavy-bottomed pot until leeks are tender.
3 eggs 1 ½ cups thickened cream sea salt & freshly ground pepper ¾ cup grated gruyère	Beat together, add leek mixture and mix well.
olive oil spray	Preheat oven to 190°C. Roll out dough and use to line a tart tin, pressing dough into sides with your finger tips. Line with a circle of lightly oiled foil and fill with dried beans. Cook in middle level of oven for 8–9 minutes until pastry is set (this is called blind baking). Remove foil and beans. Put leek mixture in pastry shell and cook in the upper part of oven for 25–30 minutes until puffed and golden. Serves 8

'A good all round shortcrust pastry which can be used for both savoury and sweet tarts.'

Artichauts Hollandaise
(Globe Artichokes with Hollandaise Sauce)

6 globe artichokes 2 lemons, halved	Snap artichoke stalks off. Trim to flush with base. Remove damaged leaves, lie on the side and slice 2 cm off tops. Trim off points of leaves with scissors. Gently spread centre leaves out and remove hairy choke with a spoon. Rub all over with lemon and drop into cold water to cover. Squeeze in more lemon juice and add lemon carcasses.
sea salt	Bring a very large pot of salted water to the boil. Add artichokes and weigh down with a plate. Cook at rapid simmer for about 30 minutes or until bottoms are tender when pierced. Drain well.
250 gm unsalted butter	While cooking, make hollandaise. To clarify butter, melt slowly in a small pot. Skim off impurities, then pour into jug leaving residue behind.
4 egg yolks 2 splashes cold water	Put in a heatproof bowl over just simmering water and whisk until thickish. Remove from heat and add the butter, little by little, whisking continually.
juice of 1 lemon sea salt & freshly ground pepper	Add to taste. Place artichokes on plates, spread leaves apart and add a dollop or two of the hollondaise sauce to the centre. Serves 6

Tolarno was the first place I visited when I returned to Melbourne, permanently, more than 30 years ago. And that visit reawakened the excitement and astonishment I had felt, on my first visit to Melbourne years earlier, at discovering a slice of the Left Bank of Paris in downtown St Kilda.

In the mid-1970s, St Kilda was a less than salubrious Melbourne suburb with working girls on every corner, seedy takeaway establishments more intent on selling strange and illicit substances than food, and a number of 'interesting' nightclubs – one of which operated proudly behind a bold sign proclaiming 'This Is The Show'. Which always made me giggle.

And in that world, Tolarno French Bistro shone like a beacon of civilisation: it was vibrant, charismatic and exciting. And the food was bloody good, to boot, and always had been.

My first meal there, eaten in the Mora years, beginning with moules marinière and continuing through steak with ratatouille and a maître d'hôtel (or was it marchand de vin) butter, followed by an excellent crème caramel, may not seem earth-shattering by today's standards, but it was pretty special, let me tell you, at a time when restaurant menus centred around surf 'n' turf, chicken Maryland and the like.

Asparagus with Double Peeled Broad Beans, Olive Oil, Balsamic & Parmesan

sea salt 3 cups broad beans, shelled	Bring a large heavy-bottomed pot of salted water to the boil. Add broad beans and bring back to boil. Drain, and when cool enough to handle, peel.
2–3 bunches gourmet (thin) asparagus, trimmed	Bring water back to boil, add asparagus and cook until crisp–tender. Drain well and share between 4 plates.
extra virgin olive oil balsamic vinegar shavings of parmesan chopped fresh Italian (flat leaf) parsley	Scatter broad beans over the top, then sprinkle with a generous amount of oil and balsamic, before topping with parmesan and parsley.
	Serves 4

Gratin de Macaroni et Maïs
(Macaroni & Corn Cheese)

sea salt 400 gm penne 3 corn cobs, kernels removed	Preheat oven to 220°C. Bring a large heavy-bottomed pot of water to rapid boil. Add salt and penne, cover, and bring back to boil as soon as possible. Uncover, stir well with a wooden spoon, and cook until al dente, adding corn for the last minute. Drain well.
2 cups Mornay Sauce, heated (page 257)	Toss with pasta and put in a large gratin dish.
4 tsp Italian tomato-based pasta sauce grated tasty cheese freshly grated parmesan	Sprinkle tomato sauce over pasta, then top with generous amount of cheese. Cook in oven until golden and bubbling.

Serves 4

'Everybody, seemingly, loves macaroni cheese – a very popular vegetarian choice when on the menu at Tolarno. We used penne rather than macaroni, purely and simply because penne allows the sauce to get inside the pasta and, let's be fair, the main reason for eating macaroni cheese is because of the wonderful, rich cheesy sauce – so no shortcuts please. (The same sauce was also used for our ever-popular Cauliflower Cheese.)'

Galette de Poisson Salé avec Aïoli
(House Salted Fish Cakes with Dijon Mustard Aïoli)

1 kilo blue eye fillets rock salt	Cover fish with salt, cover with plastic wrap and leave overnight. Next day, wash well to remove salt and put under running water for 5 minutes.
1 onion, sliced 10 juniper berries, crushed a little 2 sprigs fresh thyme 1 bay leaf milk to cover	Put fish in a deep sauté pan, add other ingredients and cover with milk. Simmer very gently until cooked, then remove fish. Whiz up fish in a processor and put in a bowl.
5 large potatoes, peeled	Boil in unsalted water until cooked. Drain and mash.
1 cup olive oil freshly ground pepper	Add oil and potato to fish and mix well. Season to taste with pepper.
plain flour ½ cup milk 2 eggs, beaten 2 cups breadcrumbs olive oil	Put flour in one bowl, milk and egg in another and crumbs in a third. Form fish mixture into cakes. Then dip in flour, egg and crumb. Heat oil in a large pan. Fry until golden and drain on kitchen paper towels.
wild rocket leaves extra virgin olive oil balsamic vinegar Dijon Mustard Aïoli (page 256) lemon wedges	Dress rocket with oil and balsamic. Place a mound on each plate, top with fish cakes and serve with a dollop of aïoli and a lemon wedge on the side. Serves 6—8

Slow-roasted Tomatoes on Sourdough with Feta

8 medium ripe, red tomatoes, cored olive oil sea salt & freshly ground pepper	Preheat oven to 180°C. Put tomatoes in a baking dish. Sprinkle generously with oil and seasonings. Cook in oven until they begin to collapse, then slip off skins.
4 thick slices of sourdough bread	Toast or grill and place tomatoes on top, along with any pan juices.
100 gm feta cheese balsamic vinegar extra virgin olive oil	Crumble feta over top and sprinkle generously with oil and balsamic. Serves 4

'This is one of Ruth Allen's favourites – a wonderful starter or even a light lunch with a green salad.'

Poireaux Grillé et Sauce Gribiche
(BBQ Leeks with a Piquant Sauce)

8–12 small leeks, cleaned & washed well sea salt	Blanch in salted water until just tender. Drain well on kitchen paper towels.
3 gherkins 1 tbsp drained & chopped capers 2 heaped tbsp chopped fresh parsley 2–3 splashes Tabasco a good splash of red wine vinegar	To make the Sauce Gribiche, whiz up in a processor, then put in a bowl.
1 cup Aïoli (page 256) 2 hard-boiled eggs, grated	Add and carefully mix in.
olive oil spray Mustard Vinaigrette (page 256)	Preheat ridged grill or BBQ. Spray leeks with oil and cook until tender and well coloured, turning every now and then. Serve with a little vinaigrette and the sauce sprinkled over the top. Serves 4

'In early days, leeks were often known as "Poor Man's Asparagus" – what a wonderful name.'

Zucchini Flowers Stuffed with a Scallop Mousseline

400 gm fresh, scallops, cleaned 2 tsp sea salt freshly ground pepper	Whiz up in a food processor.
1 egg 1 egg white	Add and mix in. Leave in processor bowl and refrigerate for 30 minutes.
155 ml thickened cream	Return bowl to processor and mix in well.
12–16 zucchini flowers, washed carefully & dried	Put scallop mixture into piping bag and, spreading flowers apart, pipe into the centre. Reform, pressing flowers back into shape.
6 cups vegetable oil batter (page 120) sea salt	Heat oil in a deep-sided pot or wok to 180°C. Without overcrowding, dip flowers into batter and fry until golden. Drain well on kitchen paper towels and salt lightly.
Hollandaise Sauce (page 53)	Serve with hollandaise on the side. Serves 6–8

'Unless the scallops are dry (not soaked in water) the dish will be a disaster.'

Soufflés à la Suissesse
(Twice Baked Cheese Soufflés)

90 gm butter 50 gm plain flour 210 ml milk	Preheat oven to 180°C. Melt butter in a heavy-bottomed pot. Add flour and cook over low heat for 2 minutes. Heat milk and add gradually, whisking continually. Simmer for 5 minutes.
50 gm gruyère, grated 25 gm freshly grated parmesan 1 small garlic clove, crushed ½ tsp olive oil	Add and mix well. Remove from heat and cool slightly.
3 large eggs, separated	Fold yolks into sauce. Then beat whites to stiff peaks and fold them in too.
melted butter	Butter 4 small soufflé or dariole moulds, spoon mixture in and smooth tops. Place folded newspaper in base of a baking dish, put moulds on top and pour boiling water to come up to two thirds of the moulds. Cook in oven until puffed and firm to the touch (about 20 minutes). Rest for a few minutes, then remove from moulds. They can be prepared ahead up to this point.
2 cups thickened cream 2 heaped tbsp mascarpone 2 heaped tbsp blue cheese a good dollop of Mornay Sauce (page 257)	Preheat oven to 220°C. Put cream and cheeses and mornay sauce in a pot and gently reduce by half. Put soufflés in a baking dish which holds them comfortably (not too large) and pour cream mixture over the top. Cook in oven until puffed and well coloured.

Serves 4

Oeufs Sur le Plat 'Florentine'
(Eggs on a Plate with Spinach)

2 good handfuls baby spinach	Preheat oven to 200°C. Remove stalks, wash well and drain. Then put in a bowl and pour boiling water to cover. Leave for 2 minutes then drain well. Squeeze excess moisture out with hands. Share between 4 small ovenproof gratin dishes.
freshly grated parmesan 8 large eggs sea salt & freshly ground pepper	Sprinkle spinach with cheese. Break eggs, one at time, into a cup and carefully put two, separately, on top of spinach. Bake for about 4 minutes until just set.
Hollandaise Sauce (page 53)	Sprinkle with hollandaise and serve immediately. Serves 4

Potato Blini with Smoked Salmon & Salmon Caviar

250 gm floury potatoes, peeled	Preheat oven to 180°C. Boil potatoes until almost cooked. Drain, place in an ovenproof dish, cover and cook in oven until tender and dry.
60 ml milk, heated	Put potatoes in a processor, along with milk and whiz until smooth. Cool for 1 hour in processor bowl.
2 eggs 35 gm potato flour 2 egg whites sea salt & freshly ground pepper	Add 1 egg and flour and process well. Then add remaining egg and whites. Blend and season. (Mixture should be consistency of a pancake batter, but may need a little more milk or flour, depending on the potatoes.)
olive oil spray	Heat a lightly oiled grill plate or non-stick frying pan. Spoon in tablespoonfuls of mixture and cook on both sides as you would a pikelet (turning once bubbles pop).
smoked salmon sour cream mixed with creamed horseradish, to taste salmon caviar	Top with smoked salmon, sour cream and salmon caviar. Serves 4

'Potato varieties suitable for this recipe include Toolangi delight, sebago and russet burbank (aka Idaho).'

Ratatouille Niçoise et Oeufs Pochés
(A Provençal Vegetable Stew with a Poached Egg)

olive oil 1 red onion, cut into thin wedges 2 garlic cloves, crushed	Heat a little oil in a heavy-bottomed pot and sauté until tender.
2 zucchini, diced 1 medium eggplant, diced 1 red capsicum, cored, seeded & diced 1 green capsicum, cored, seeded & diced	Add, mix well and cook gently for 10 minutes, tossing regularly.
2 x 400 gm cans diced tomatoes, drained a little ½ cup vegetable stock, bought (low salt) or homemade (page 254)	Add and cook down until thick and fragrant.
3 anchovy fillets, chopped 12 black olives, pitted 1 tbsp chopped fresh basil	Add, mix in and briefly cook. Mound ratatouille in bowls.
white vinegar 4 eggs	Bring a deep sauté pan of water to the boil. Add a splash of vinegar and swirl vigorously with a spoon. Slide in eggs and cook over gentle heat. Put on top of ratatouille.

Serves 4

Crème Crécy
(Cream of Carrot Soup)

a good knob of butter 6 medium carrots, peeled & chopped 1 large brown onion, peeled & chopped 3 medium potatoes, peeled & chopped	Heat butter in a heavy-bottomed pot and sauté gently for 5 minutes.
1 ½ litres chicken stock, bought (low salt) or homemade (page 254) sea salt & freshly ground pepper	Add and simmer until very tender, then blend until smooth. Return to pot.
100 gm butter a good slurp of thickened cream	Add and simmer to incorporate. Ladle into bowls.
sour cream 1 roasted red capsicum (see below), cut into strips snipped fresh chives	Top with a dollop of sour cream, scatter over capsicum and chives and serve. Serves 6

'I would love you to try this – I know Cream of Carrot Soup doesn't sound that inspiring but this is fantastic. And to roast capsicum, simply roast or grill it until until brown-black all over. Then cover with a roasting tray or tea towel until cool, then core, seed and peel.'

Garbure
(A Hearty Winter Soup from the Basque Region)

2 medium carrots, peeled & cut into thickish slices 2 large celery stalks, cut into thickish slices 1 large onion, chopped 1 smoked pork hock 1 x 250 gm piece rindless bacon 3 litres chicken stock, bought (low salt) or homemade (page 254)	Put in a pot and cover with stock. Bring to simmer and cook gently for 1 hour, adding more stock as needed. Remove meat and set aside. When cool enough to handle, remove skin and sinew and chop evenly.
8–12 baby potatoes, peeled & halved 3 chorizo sausages	While meat is cooling, add to liquid and cook gently until potatoes are almost tender. Remove chorizo and chop.
1 x 375 gm can cannellini beans, drained & rinsed ½ savoy cabbage, finely shredded, all ribs removed	Add along with chopped meats and cook until cabbage is tender.
slices of baguette olive oil spray	Preheat oven to 180°C. While soup is cooking make croutons. Spray baguette slices with olive oil and cook in oven until golden.
Aïoli (page 256)	Serve croutons on top of soup with a good dollop of aïoli. Serves 8–10

Soupe au Pistou
(A Provençal Vegetable Soup with Basil)

olive oil 2 leeks, washed well & diced 2 celery stalks, diced 1 large potato, peeled & diced 2 medium carrots, peeled & diced 1 medium fennel bulb, cored & diced	Heat a little oil in a large heavy-bottomed pot and sauté gently until tender.
2 litres chicken or vegetable stock, bought (low salt) or homemade (page 254) 2 cups soup pasta 1 x 400 gm can diced tomatoes, drained a little sea salt & freshly ground pepper	Add and cook until pasta is al dente, adding more stock if needed.
1 x 375 gm can cannellini beans, drained & rinsed 1 cup frozen peas, thawed 2 medium zucchini, diced Basil Pistou (page 257)	Add along with the pistou to taste and cook for 5 minutes or so.

Serves 6–8

'This is, of course, the Provençal version of minestrone.'

Crème Vichyssoise Glacée
(Chilled Leek & Potato Soup)

4 large potatoes, peeled & chopped 4 large onions, peeled & chopped 4 leeks, washed well & chopped 1.5 litres chicken stock, bought (low salt) or homemade (page 254) sea salt & freshly ground white pepper	Put in a large heavy-bottomed pot and cook until very tender. Then, whiz up in a blender in 3 or 4 lots. Cool a little.
½ – ¾ cup thickened cream 4 tbsp snipped chives	Add, whisk well and check seasoning. (Remember seasoning needs to be more aggressive in food that is to be served cold.) Chill thoroughly.

Serves 6

'This, the most famous of all chilled soups, was created by Louis Diat from New York's Ritz-Carlton. Looking for a cold soup, he remembered how his mother used to chill down her leek and potato soup on a warm day by adding cold cream or milk to it. He named it after Vichy, the spa near his home, and 'voila', a classic was born.'

Snow Pea Soup with a Splash of Champagne

5 large potatoes, peeled & chopped 5 large onions, peeled & chopped 1.5 litres chicken stock, bought (low salt) or homemade (page 254) sea salt & freshly ground pepper	Put in a large heavy-bottomed pot and cook until very tender. (Can be done in advance up to this point.)
1 kilo snow or sugar snap peas, topped & tailed 2 cups frozen peas, thawed	Add, all at once, to rapidly boiling mixture. The second it comes back to boil, turn off and quickly blend in 2 or 3 lots. Check seasoning and put into bowls.
French champagne	At the table, add a splash of champagne to each bowl. Serves 6

'This originally featured at one of my other restaurants, Fleurie. Years later Emma Mackay (who had done her apprenticeship at Tolarno under Leon) admitted that she always helped herself to a glass before the champagne went to the table. At Tolarno, to negate this I personally sent it out, but then again was not averse to helping myself to a glass too.'

Soupe à l'Oignon Gratinée
(Cheese Gratinéed French Onion Soup)

4 tbsp olive oil 1 kilo brown onions, sliced	Heat oil in a heavy-bottomed pot and sauté, until dark brown, stirring regularly. Start off on high heat and turn down as the cooking progresses.
4 tbsp plain flour	Add and mix well. Cook over low heat for 5 minutes, stirring continually.
1.5 litres beef stock, bought (low salt) or homemade (page 254) 250 ml dry white wine sea salt & freshly ground pepper	Add and whisk well. Simmer for 30–40 minutes. Check seasoning.
3–4 slices day-old sandwich bread, crusts removed olive oil	Cut bread into 2 cm croutons. Heat oil in a pan and fry croutons until golden brown on both sides. Drain well on kitchen paper towels.
brandy grated tasty cheese freshly grated parmesan	Preheat overhead grill. Put a splash of brandy in each bowl and add soup. Top with croutons to cover, then a thick layer of tasty cheese. Add some parmesan and grill until golden and bubbling.

Serves 6–8

'Although onion soup itself originates in Lyon, where the onion is a champion, it was in Les Halles—the markets of Paris—where Soupe à l'Oignon Gratinée first appeared. More of a meal than a snack, the market workers began adding the remnants of their wine or cognac glasses and this hearty wonderful bistro staple was born as we know it today. But one word of warning: true onion soup is thick and covered in cheese; not stock with a few onions and a small croûte floating on top (as we have seen over the years in many Aussie restaurants).'

Soupe Cultivateur
(The Farmer's Vegetable Soup)

olive oil 1 large onion, chopped 1 large leek, washed well & finely diced 1 medium carrot, diced 2 celery stalks, diced 2 garlic cloves, crushed 1 x 2 cm piece rindless bacon, cut into lardons (page 193)	Heat oil in a heavy-bottomed pot and sauté, gently, until tender.
2 large potatoes, diced ½ butternut pumpkin, diced 1 x 400 gm can diced tomatoes, drained a little chicken stock bought or homemade (page 254) sea salt & freshly ground pepper	Add, making sure stock covers ingredients by 2 cm, and simmer until very tender.
100 gm small pasta	Add and continue to cook until pasta is tender.
2 tbsp Basil Pistou (page 257) baguette	Add, mix in and serve with lots of crusty baguette. Serves 6

'You can, of course, vary the vegetables to suit the season. And you can, if you like, substitute well-drained and rinsed canned beans (such as cannelloni or haricot) for the pasta.'

Mirka Mora was, and still is, both mischievous and saucy. And on a quiet night in Tolarno – Georges was abroad but painter Charles Blackman, Mirka's old partner in crime, was on hand to help her keep an eye on things – she wickedly combined both of these aspects of her character.

'I was wearing a black velvet top in which I cut two little holes where my nipples were, and I let them out. I thought it would be fun to see how customers reacted when they came to pay their bills,' Mirka told me, years later.

Most customers, she claimed, pretended not to notice, while some looked very carefully indeed – initially, in disbelief. She and Charles then began to assess customers according to their reaction to Mirka's nipples and, as each group left, howled with laughter.

But while the vast majority chose, after a time, to look elsewhere – some even finding something very fascinating about their own feet – one middle-aged man was transfixed by the nipple show, and stared at them intently. Until, of course, his wife noticed his interest and belted him across the ear with her handbag.

Whereupon he paid the bill, still staring at the perky protuberances, and left. But Mirka insists, for the life of her, that she cannot remember whether or not he tipped.

The MASSONI Years

While most Melburnians, even in 1974, were reckoned to have fairly conventional red blood flowing through their veins, Leon Massoni almost certainly had red wine with a touch of garlic, some melted butter, a dollop of cream, a splash of olive oil and perhaps a hint of champagne vinegar flowing through his. Because when it came to food and restaurants, pursuits in which he had immersed himself for most of his life, Leon was both passionate and pernickety. With Leon in charge, no idea would be left unexplored, no opportunity missed, no detail allowed to go unattended. If there was anything that Leon did not know about restaurants by the 1970s, it was, quite simply, not worth knowing.

'When the price of tomatoes increased by two cents in the market, Leon would review the menu and adjust the prices accordingly,' insists William Mora, who in his late teens and early twenties had run Tolarno French Bistro for the closing years of the Mora era. As the 1970s unfolded, Georges became increasingly preoccupied with his art gallery business, while Mirka moved into a studio in Wellington Street, St Kilda, having, in 1970, reluctantly separated from Georges and, to a lesser extent, her three sons, to devote her life to painting.

'My appointment to the manager role just happened,' explains William. 'One day, Georges told me he had to travel – something he did regularly although, on that occasion, it was to leave Mum in peace while she moved out of Tolarno into a studio in nearby Wellington Street – and that I was in charge. And he gave me the keys. Just like that.'

'By that time, Georges had sold the freehold to the building, and the hotel operation, to cover his debts, retaining only a lease on the ground floor. There is no doubt that he had his eye more firmly on the gallery and on fine art than on Tolarno French Bistro.'

But Leon Massoni, mercifully, was waiting in the wings, and was more than ready to return to the restaurant game after some initially promising but ultimately unsatisfactory years in the wine trade. It was Leon's father, Rinaldo, after all, who had taught Melbourne most of what it then knew about fine dining by, in 1928, creating the glorious Café Florentino in Bourke Street. Leon had grown up in the Flo and had run it, brilliantly, for sixteen years after his father's death before selling it in 1962 to try his luck in wine.

And so it was that as the 1970s dawned and Tolarno French Bistro struggled to compensate for the defection of Mirka, its artistic soul, and the dwindling commitment of Georges, its creator, something of a slide began for the place that had meant so much for so long to so many. In 1974, just ten years after the Mora fairytale had begun, Leon stepped in and, with Georges' blessing and probably to Georges' profound relief, took charge. Tolarno French Bistro, suddenly, belonged to Leon Massoni, and a brilliant new era dawned.

'I didn't have to buy it from Georges,' says Leon. 'No money changed hands. We simply had an arrangement under which I walked in and took it over. Just like that.

'I knew how things were going with Tolarno because in those days, a report was widely circulated about the performances of all wine licences in Victoria. And I could see that Tolarno wine sales were going down and down. I think Georges was very relieved when I appeared on the scene. The place was going broke, and he happily assigned the lease to me.

'When we took over, the patrons had virtually disappeared and the restaurant was empty. Everything was still in place, and everything was functioning, but there was no business. The place had lost its momentum, the customers had lost interest, and Georges had lost his passion for the place. He was always there, in body at least, but that was about it.

'Also, the place was very, very grubby and tired. The first thing we had to do was to give it a really good clean and to reconfigure the entrance, just to show that there was a new game in town.

'And the extraordinary thing was that by our second night in business, the place was full again. And it stayed full until the day we left. We were open seven days a week, lunch and dinner. And I loved every minute of it.'

Like Georges before him, Leon strengthened his battle lines at Tolarno by recruiting from his immediate family. He was joined at Tolarno by David Gibson, his step-son – first as a casual employee during

⊕ Chef Louis Ercout and Leon Massoni

⊕ Leon outside Tolarno in the 1970s

Saturday lunches and on occasional nights, and eventually as a partner and key member of Leon's Tolarno French Bistro team.

Leon's stewardship of Tolarno French Bistro was bursting with masterstrokes. But perhaps the most important of these was the way in which he demonstrated just how serious he was about fine food by staffing the place, for its rebirth, with not one, but two outstanding Melbourne chefs.

One was Pietro Grossi, Italian; the other, Jim Fatsouros, Greek. But the food? Unapologetically French, of course – the food around which both chefs, in finest European tradition, had completed their training. Leon provided the classic recipes and his chefs did the rest, and to extraordinary effect. Through the Massoni era, Tolarno food soared about as high as bistro food had ever soared in Australia.

There had, of course, been a small brigade in place when Leon took charge. But he knew that if he was to lift the bistro out of the doldrums, and open for the additional hours – the place was closed on Mondays and for Saturday lunches in the Mora years – he would need more kitchen firepower. So he installed the two veteran chefs, the Italian and the Greek, in whom he had absolute confidence.

'Those two chefs could impart more flavour into the food they cooked than any chefs I have ever known,' says Leon which, when you consider the chefs he has known and employed, is quite a recommendation. Menu offerings remained within the bistro repertoire and the best-sellers, as Leon remembers clearly, were moules marinière, coquille St Jacques, onion soup (gratinée, naturally), steak tartare, boeuf à la bourguignonne, coq au vin and, naturally, chocolate mousse.

'There were a lot of old Florentino customers who, when they heard I had taken over Tolarno, came there to eat. But there was one problem with that: a signature dish at Flo had been chocolate soufflés and when they came to Tolarno, they all ordered chocolate soufflés. But somehow, dessert soufflés just didn't work in the casual atmosphere of a bistro, and neither of the chefs were comfortable about preparing them. So the customers had to settle for chocolate mousse.'

Fortunately for those customers, Mirka was no longer a fixture at Tolarno which

meant, also, that no longer was chocolate mousse flicked across the room with deadly accuracy by an artist wielding a parfait spoon. Not in the Massoni era. Never. Not with Leon around. Or at least, not by anyone who valued their job or, for that matter, their life.

David Gibson played an increasingly pivotal role on several fronts. In the early years, David remembers, one of his responsibilities was to drive to Port Melbourne early in the day to buy freshly caught snapper from a local fisherman. Or to drive to St Kilda Pier to collect a box or two of still-flapping local flounder, for $1 a pop. And the freshness of the fish at Tolarno was something mentioned in many of the written assessments of the place, and often marvelled at by customers – 'especially those from the country who would tell me they had no idea fish could taste like that,' says David.

But later, David's focus shifted to working on the business rather than in the business: years before many restaurants had thought of it. David fully computerised Leon's operation, allowing his step-father to make the last-minute price adjustments to his menu – the adjustments that had so fascinated William Mora who had for years watched his father toss the day's paperwork into a jar and fold the takings into his pocket. The business was changing …

And with a change in operator for the iconic bistro as well as a change in business practices came, inevitably, a change in the profile of customers. There was a degree of continuity or, rather, some renewed interest from old customers who had all but given up on the place. Some artists still came but were required to pay for their meals under Leon's regime, which struck some of them as unsporting. And as the Tolarno Gallery behind the restaurant continued to operate, and to prosper, with William working closely with Georges, there was still support from the arts community.

Politicians returned, as did Melbourne establishment figures and members of the squattocracy. But another group of returning 'regulars' came from St Kilda Road, from the booming ad agencies. These were the new creatives – bohemians in Beemers, with extravagant expense accounts. These, also, were the years of the very long lunch, which suited Leon fine. It was only when the admen wanted to add the evening shift to their luncheon outings that problems arose because the bistro, inevitably, was booked solid for dinner, probably for sittings at 6 pm, and again at 8 pm. Those were the days before fringe benefits tax, naturally.

It should be remembered, however, that while this era of Tolarno is seen as marking the beginnings of the gentrification of Fitzroy Street, life in St Kilda was still raw. Rooms in the area were rented by the hour and the stocky, businesslike women of a certain age who had formerly worked the streets of St Kilda were gradually making way, in the 1970s, for younger, prettier but druggier women in the same profession.

'We used to marvel at how hard some of these girls worked and, occasionally, we would keep count of the number of customers they would bring back to Tolarno in a day,' recalls Leon. 'The record, I think, was seventeen. And a lovely-looking girl it was who set the mark, too.'

The ground floor Tolarno toilets also saw their share of the street action: a working girl would occasionally slip past Leon and enter the ladies', dragging a desperate client behind her. More seriously, girls would occasionally overdose in those same toilets.

Leon, in fact, was outraged by the fact that all too often, undercover police officers would dine extravagantly in Tolarno without ever paying for the food and wine they consumed. They were keeping an eye on things, they would insist. But curiously, those complimentary meals never seemed to result in police action of any kind – certainly nothing as dramatic as an arrest.

Violence, also, despite the well-fed and ever-present arm of the law, remained part of the streetscape, as Leon well remembers: 'One night, just on 1 am, I heard what sounded like a shot outside, just as I was locking up. I checked and, sure enough, it had been a very good one, apparently, because the victim lay dead in the gutter. I stayed inside.'

On another occasion, Leon was attacked by a man armed with a nunchaku just metres from the front door of the restaurant.

'I was carrying payroll money, and he was obviously aware of this. He hit me across the back of the head and tried to take the money from me. I held on tight to the money and managed to kick him in the balls, and he ran off. Or limped off, anyway. He was later arrested by police officers who had seen the entire incident from a nearby balcony,' says Leon, who never did discover what the police, who had appeared to be breathless even before they began their chase, were actually doing on that balcony.

While the focus of Tolarno remained the front room which held 54 patrons and was generally full-to-bursting during the Massoni years, Leon saw a further possibility – one that has been vital to the continuing financial health of Tolarno.

In space facing Fitzroy Street, but on the opposite side of the entrance hallway to the bistro, an area occupied by an independent operation called Pancake Zoo, Leon opened Tolarno Two–Brochettes, a contemporary grill room offering, as the name implied, charcoal-seared brochettes of lamb, chicken, beef, pork, seafood and so on. And that place, too, was a sensation.

As David Gibson remembers, Brochettes, in addition to the following it quickly developed, served as a useful overspill for Tolarno French Bistro.

'You have to remember that the bistro was licensed to accommodate only 54 diners at a time. But every week, we would serve between 1500 and 1600 meals. Tolarno was full all the time,' says David.

But one of the reasons for the success of Brochettes, according to Leon, was a familiar one: Mirka, who had remained close to Tolarno, and to both Leon and his wife, Vivienne, returned to create an exquisite piece of art, one of her very best pieces, along a bare wall in the new space.

'She created something she called a plaster flurry – a typical Mirka design, but three-dimensional. It was quite stunning,' declares Leon. And like most Mirka contributions to the place, not to mention the artist herself, it is still stunning, much valued and deeply loved.

Not that every piece of artwork Mirka undertook for the Massonis was as successful: there was also the painting that she was commissioned to paint for the gentlemen's lavatory – a painting that, after much soul-searching and due consideration Leon and Vivienne nervously returned to Mirka.

'She took it quite well, but I am sure she thought we were both very square,' says

Vivienne. 'But really, it was just too much for us.'

Too much? Mirka is still puzzled by this perception. Because her large painting was, after all, a perfectly splendid rendition of a huge phallus, in the pink of condition, suitably entwined with flowers. Just the sort of thing every right-thinking gentlemen's lavatory should contain, in Mirka's opinion.

Inevitably, Leon Massoni's impeccable stewardship of Tolarno was another of those things which, sadly, could not last forever. And in June 1988, he sold it, sentencing the place to three years of sad obscurity and mediocrity that few people, mercifully, can even remember: we shall not even try. Suffice to say, it was purchased by two businessmen who had no understanding of what the restaurant was all about and endeavoured to alter both the food and the approach and to shape the place into something for which there was, quite simply, no demand in Fitzroy Street. But to their credit, they did little lasting damage to the interior: all but one of Mirka's magical images survived, and would soon have more work on their hands, more spells to weave.

It was less than three years after that sale that veteran Melbourne food writer Claude Forell wrote in *The Age* newspaper of the once bustling, now sadly neglected lady of Fitzroy Street which, in Claude's words, 'was in need of new owners willing and able to restore it to its former charm, quality and popularity'.

Claude called Mirka Mora, naturally.

'If I were not a painter I would come back tomorrow to reopen it,' she told him. 'I miss the restaurant very much.'

Claude also called Leon Massoni who, at a sprightly 65, described the bistro's reduced circumstances as 'a bloody shame', suggesting that it needed someone with 'vigour and vitality' to recapture the magic. But not him.

But waiting in the wings, this time, was a man who had shown himself to be one of Melbourne's most innovative and important restaurateurs of the era – a Kiwi chef called Iain Hewitson. He had the 'vigour and vitality' Leon had specified, a healthy respect for Tolarno's history as well as a deep affection for the place. And as luck would have it, Huey, who was as deeply involved with the restaurant business as ever, was prepared to place himself between engagements ...

→ Leon's image presided over diners in Mirka's Salon right through the Hewitson-Allen years

THE MASSONI YEARS

Fricassée de Poulet 'Waterzooi'
Poulet Grillé à la Diable
Coq au Vin
Poulet en Cocotte Bonne Femme
Poulet Basquaise
Poulet Sauté à l'Estragon
Confit de Caneton
Caneton à l'Orange
*Tagine of Duck Confit, Lamb Kefta
& Merguez Sausage in Harissa Broth*
Brochettes de Foie de Caneton
Caneton en Casserole

POULTRY

'Bistro fare is not afraid to be lusty and earthy, filling the air with wafts of pungent garlic or sweet bacon sizzling in a huge steel skillet.'
Patricia Wells
Bistro Cooking, 1989

Fricassée de Poulet 'Waterzooi'
(Flemish Stewed Chicken)

4 chicken marylands 2 sprigs fresh parsley 6 whole black peppercorns 2 bay leaves 3 thick slices lemon chicken stock, bought (low salt) or homemade (page 254)	Put everything in a pot and cover with stock. Simmer very, very gently for 20 or so minutes until chicken is just cooked. Strain, reserving stock, and, when cool enough to handle, skin and slice chicken flesh.
unsalted butter 1 medium onion, finely chopped 3 leeks, washed well & cut into thin rounds 1 celery stalk, diced	While chicken is cooking, melt a few knobs of butter and sauté vegetables until tender.
1 tbsp plain flour sea salt & freshly ground pepper ¼ cup thickened cream	Add flour, mix well and cook over low heat for a few minutes, stirring. Then add poaching liquid and whisk well. Check seasoning, add cream and cook gently for 10 minutes.
2 tbsp chopped fresh chervil 2 egg yolks (optional)	Return chicken and toss to reheat. Then add chervil. Beat yolks and, off the heat, mix through.
pasta or egg noodles	Serve on cooked pasta or noodles.

Serves 4

Poulet Grillé à la Diable
(Devilled Chicken)

1 large chicken	Preheat oven to 200°C. Cut out backbone using kitchen scissors. Turn over and flatten breastbone with a few blows from the palm of the hand. Tuck wings under and then skewer chicken by pushing metal skewers crossways through wings, then body and then thighs and drumsticks. Repeat process on the other side with a second skewer. Put on an oven tray.
Garlic Butter (page 48) ½ lemon sea salt & freshly ground pepper	Melt some garlic butter and brush all over chicken. Squeeze lemon juice over top and season well. Cook in oven for about 45 minutes until juices run clear when you press a fork into thigh.
Dijon mustard breadcrumbs garlic butter, melted	Preheat overhead grill. Brush chicken all over with mustard, then sprinkle with crumbs. Baste with extra garlic butter and cook under grill until golden. Portion into 4.
fresh watercress olive oil balsamic vinegar	Toss watercress with oil and balsamic and serve alongside.

Serves 4

Coq au Vin
(Chicken in Red Wine)

1 large chicken, portioned into 4 1 onion, diced 1 medium carrot, peeled & sliced 1 celery stalk, sliced 1 tbsp whole black peppercorns 750 ml red wine	Combine, cover and refrigerate overnight.
olive oil sea salt & freshly ground pepper	Remove chicken, reserving marinade, pat dry and season. Heat oil in a deep sauté pan and brown chicken all over. Remove.
olive oil 1 x 2 cm piece of rindless bacon, cut into lardons (page 193) 12–16 baby pickling onions, peeled 12–16 button mushrooms, wiped	Wipe out pan. Add some fresh oil and sauté until lightly coloured.
1 heaped tbsp plain flour	Add, mix well and cook for a few minutes over low heat.
3 cups chicken stock, bought (low salt) or homemade (page 254) 200 gm canned diced tomatoes, drained a little	Add along with strained marinade and mix well. Cook until lightly thickened. Return chicken to pan and simmer, turning a few times, until cooked.
chopped fresh parsley	Serve sprinkled with parsley. Serves 4

Poulet en Cocotte Bonne Femme
(Chicken in a Pot with Bacon, Onions & Mushrooms)

olive oil 1 large chicken, portioned into 4	Heat oil in a heavy-bottomed casserole. Brown chicken all over and remove.
2 tbsp butter 1 x 2 cm thick piece of rindless bacon, cut into lardons (page 193) 12 baby pickling onions, peeled 12 button mushrooms, wiped with a damp cloth	Add butter to casserole and sauté ingredients until lightly coloured.
2 tbsp plain flour 3 + cups chicken stock, bought (low salt) or homemade (page 254) 2 tbsp chopped fresh parsley sea salt & freshly ground pepper	Add flour and cook over gentle heat stirring frequently. Then add 3 cups stock and the parsley and whisk well. Season to taste, return chicken to pan and cover. Simmer very gently for about 30 minutes until cooked through, turning chicken every now and then, adding more stock if needed.

Serves 4

Poulet Basquaise
(Braised Chicken with Capsicum, Pancetta & Tomato)

olive oil 1 large chicken, portioned into 4	Heat a thin layer of oil in a deep-sided sauté pan. Add chicken, cover pan and brown all over. Remove.
3 garlic cloves, crushed 3 chillies, sliced 4 slices pancetta, diced 1 large red onion, cut into thin wedges 1 large red capsicum, cored, seeded & sliced 1 large yellow capsicum, cored, seeded & sliced	Add, along with more oil if needed, and sauté until tender.
2 x 400 gm cans diced tomatoes, drained a little ½ cup dry white wine 2 cups chicken stock, bought (low salt) or homemade (page 254) sea salt & freshly ground pepper	Add, mix well and bring to the boil. Turn down to simmer, return chicken and cook, covered, turning two or three times.
12–15 fresh basil leaves, torn	Add and cook briefly. Check seasoning.

Serves 4

'The early Tolarno menus featured Chicken Provençale. I seem to remember it having a good whack of chilli, so I believe it was more likely to be the Basque variation rather than the simple, rather basic number from Provence.'

Poulet Sauté a l'Estragon
(Sautéed Chicken with Tarragon)

olive oil 1 large chicken, portioned into 4, skin on plain flour sea salt & freshly ground pepper	Heat a layer of oil in a deep sauté pan. Flour chicken lightly, season and cook, covered, until golden all over.
½ cup tarragon vinegar	Add and reduce by one-third.
2–3 cups chicken stock, bought (low salt) or homemade (page 254) sea salt & freshly ground pepper	Add, turn down heat and simmer, turning once or twice, until cooked. Remove chicken.
a good dollop of butter 3 tbsp chopped fresh tarragon leaves	Add to sauce and cook for a few minutes. Check seasoning and pour over chicken.
Creamed Spinach (page 200)	Serve with creamed spinach on the side.

Serves 4

'A dish that should feature on every halfway decent bistro menu – it certainly does in France.'

Confit de Caneton
(Duck Cooked in its Own Fat)

4 duck marylands sea salt & freshly ground pepper	Preheat oven to 100°C. Trim marylands and toss with seasonings. Put in a deep baking dish.
3 sprigs fresh thyme 5 garlic cloves, peeled 3–4 cups duck fat, melted	Top with thyme and garlic and pour over duck fat to cover. Cook gently in oven for 2 hours. Then cool and refrigerate at least overnight.
8 baby potatoes, well scrubbed & halved sea salt & freshly ground pepper	When ready to serve, preheat oven to 250°C. Put potatoes in roasting tray and toss with seasoning and a little of the duck fat. Roast until almost tender. Then scrape fat from duck, add to tray and cook in oven for 10 minutes, turning once and pouring off excess fat as needed.
2–3 handfuls frisée lettuce Mustard Vinaigrette (page 256)	When duck is crispy and potatoes are tender, toss potatoes with lettuce and vinaigrette. Mound onto 4 plates and top with duck. Serves 4

'Another true bistro classic.'

Caneton à l'Orange
(Duck with Orange Sauce)

2 large ducks	Remove necks, gizzards etc. Puncture the skin many times with a thin skewer and pour boiling water over top. Put on a rack over a tray and refrigerate uncovered overnight. (This crisps the skin.)
1 tbsp vegetable oil 1 onion, sliced 1 carrot, sliced 2 litres chicken stock, bought (low salt) or homemade (page 254) 4 sprigs fresh parsley 1 bay leaf	At same time, cut bits and pieces of ducks into 2 cm pieces. Heat oil in a pot and brown along with the vegetables. Add stock and herbs and simmer gently for 1 hour. Cool, strain into a bowl and refrigerate overnight. Then degrease.
olive oil sea salt & freshly ground pepper	The next day, preheat oven to 220°C. Rub duck with oil and season. Cook in oven on a rack over a tray for 1 hour. When cool, remove legs and breasts. Turn oven up to 240°C, return duck and cook, skin side up for 10 minutes or so, until crispy.
4 tbsp sugar 150 ml red wine vinegar	While duck is roasting, cook in a heavy-bottomed pot until dark caramel. Add reserved stock and simmer until incorporated.
50 gm arrowroot 4 tbsp port	Mix together, add to sauce and cook until slightly thickened.
Grand Marnier blanched orange zest	Add to taste.
fresh orange segments	Add. Place either one or two pieces of the duck on each plate, arrange orange segments around and spoon sauce over top.

Serves 4–8

Tagine of Duck Confit, Lamb Kefta & Merguez Sausage in Harissa Broth

2 red onions, quartered
2 garlic cloves, halved
2 cinnamon sticks
1 tsp cracked black pepper
½ tsp saffron threads
2 tbsp harissa, bought or homemade (page 256)
2 litres beef stock, bought or homemade (page 254)

Preheat oven to 210°C.
Put in a pot and bring to the boil. Simmer until reduced by one-third. Then strain, discarding solids.

---

olive oil
½ onion, finely chopped
2 garlic cloves, crushed
250 gm minced lamb
2 heaped tbsp plain yoghurt
1 heaped tsp sambal oelek
1 tsp sweet paprika
1 tsp ground cumin
2 tbsp chopped fresh coriander
sea salt & freshly ground pepper

To make lamb kefta, heat a little oil in a pan and sauté onion and garlic until tender. Put in a bowl, add remaining ingredients and mix well. Roll into 6–12 meatballs and cook in oven on an oiled baking tray until lightly browned and firm to the touch.

---

6 Merguez sausages

Blanch in just simmering water until firmish when squeezed. Remove and set aside.

---

6 duck leg confit (page 96)
1–2 zucchini, cut in chunks
1 medium carrot, cut in chunks
harissa
couscous (page 257)

When ready to serve, put confit and sausages in oven and cook until golden, pouring off excess fat. Bring broth to boil in a deep pan, add vegetables and kefta and gently simmer until vegetables are very tender. Reheat couscous in microwave and mound in bowls. Top with confit, sausage, kefta and vegetables. Pour hot broth over and serve with harissa on the side.

Serves 6

Brochettes de Foie de Caneton
(Duck Liver Skewers)

2 garlic cloves, crushed 1 heaped tsp harissa, bought or homemade (page 256) juice of 1 lemon ½ cup olive oil sea salt & freshly ground pepper	Mix well.
16 duck livers, cleaned & halved	Add, toss and refrigerate for 30 minutes.
4 spring (green) onions, cut into 3 cm lengths	Preheat ridged grill or BBQ. Skewer livers with spring onions crossways and then grill, brushing with marinade as you do so.
steamed rice Garlic Butter (page 48)	Serve on a bed of rice with dollops of garlic butter on top. Serves 4

'I don't know whether Tolarno Two–Brochettes used harissa in the marinade for their liver brochettes, but I remember them having a nice spicy hit.'

Caneton en Casserole
(Braised Duck in a Casserole)

8 duck marylands olive oil a knob of butter	Preheat oven to 160°C. Prick duck all over with a skewer. Heat oil and butter in a heavy-bottomed casserole and brown duck on both sides, skin-side down first. Remove.
1 x 2 cm piece of rindless bacon, cut into lardons (page 193) 1 large carrot, diced 1 large onion, chopped 2 celery stalks, diced 2 garlic cloves, crushed	Pour off most of the oil, add and gently sauté until tender.
2 cups red wine a good splash of brandy	Add and reduce by half.
1 x 400 gm can diced tomatoes, drained a little 1 cup chicken stock, bought (low salt) or homemade (page 254) sea salt & freshly ground pepper	Add tomatoes and stock and bring to the boil. Check seasoning, return duck and cover with baking paper and then the lid. Cook for 1 ½ hours or so until very tender.
a good knob of butter Parsnip Mash (page 209)	Remove duck and reduce sauce over high heat, adding butter towards the end. Serve duck on parsnip mash and ladle sauce over the top. Serves 4

Coquilles St Jacques à la Provençale
Bourride
Moules Marinière
Moules à la Portugaise
Homard à la Parisienne
Bouillabaisse de Crabe
Les Crêpes aux Fruits de Mer
Crevettes à l'Ail
Quenelles de Langouste aux Épinards et Sauce Rouge
Roasted Morton Bay Bugs, Beurre Maitre d'Hôtel
John Dory with a Lemon & Caper Butter
Saumon Grillé et Sauce Vierge
Fish 'n' Chips
Truite aux Amandes
Thon Marmitako
Snapper with Pistou Mash, Parmesan & Brown Butter
Filet de Merlan Meuniere

FROM THE SEA

'It is important for each of us to make our own observations and come to our own conclusions, but I do want you to understand that cooking should be simple; there is no need to go to extremes. You are not competing for a world champion title, nor are you passing an exam. Don't feel guilty if you fail at making a Sole Meuniere once or twice, that's part of the culinary training.'
Guy Savoy
Simple French Recipes for
the Home Cook, 2004

Coquilles St Jacques à la Provençale
(Scallops in the Style of Provence)

1 punnet cherry tomatoes, halved 3 garlic cloves, peeled olive oil sea salt & freshly ground pepper	Preheat oven to 180°C. Put tomatoes and garlic in a baking tray and toss with oil and seasoning. Cook in oven until tomatoes collapse a little.
½ cup extra virgin olive oil 2 garlic cloves, crushed 3 anchovies	Heat oil in a pan and sauté garlic and anchovies until anchovies melt.
½ cup fresh sourdough breadcrumbs, made from 2-day-old bread 1 heaped tbsp chopped fresh parsley	Add and cook, stirring, until crumbs are golden. Set aside.
unsalted butter	When tomatoes are ready, remove and mash garlic and return to tray with a few good dollops of butter. Toss well to incorporate, keep warm.
16 large fresh scallops in the shell olive oil spray	Remove scallops from shells and clean. Spray a grill plate or pan and quickly sear scallops over high heat for 1–2 minutes on each side. Return to shells, divide shells between 4 plates then scatter tomato mixture over the top. Sprinkle generously with crumbs and serve.

Serves 4

'Our method of cooking scallops has certainly changed over the years. The original Scallops Provençale, as featured on early Tolarno menus, would most probably have involved them being cooked for at least 5 minutes before being bunged into the oven for another 5 minutes or so. Dare I say it, this version is an improvement.'

Bourride
(A Seafood Stew with Garlic Mayonnaise)

olive oil 1–2 small leeks, washed well & sliced 2 garlic cloves, crushed	Heat oil in a deep-sided sauté pan and sauté until tender.
1 cup dry white wine 1 cup fish stock, bought (low salt) or homemade (page 255)	Add and boil for 5 minutes.
4 x 80 gm white fish fillets (blue eye or similar) 4 x 80 gm salmon fillets 16 mussels, scrubbed & de-bearded (page 108) 2 bay leaves	Place on top, cover, and cook very gently. Remove fish as it's cooked and mussels as they open, and place in deep bowls. Discard any mussels that don't open.
1 squid tube, cleaned & cut into rings 8 large oysters, freshly shucked	When almost ready, add for 1 minute. Then place on top of fish in bowls.
a good slurp of thickened cream 2 tbsp chopped fresh parsley	Add to liquid and boil rapidly, for a minute or two.
½ cup Aïoli (page 256)	Put in a bowl and, whisking continually, adding pan contents little by little. Pour over seafood and serve.

Serves 4

Moules Marinière
(Mussels in a White Wine Broth)

1 kilo mussels, scrubbed & de-bearded (page 108) ¼ red onion, finely chopped ¼ cup dry white wine 2 tbsp chopped fresh parsley 1 garlic clove, crushed freshly ground pepper	Put in a large wok, cover, and cook over high heat until mussels begin to open. Remove as they open and put in 2 bowls. Discard any that don't open.
thickened cream	Add a good splash of cream to the liquid. Boil for a minute or two, then pour over the mussels.
baguette	Serve with plenty of crusty bread.

Serves 2

'Before mussel farms, one of the few Melbourne restaurants that regularly featured mussels was Tolarno. Georges Mora had a friend who often brought a big bag of the blessed things in the back door – and many a customer got into the habit of ringing first and enquiring whether mussels were on the menu that day.'

Moules à la Portugaise
(Mussels in the Portuguese Style)

olive oil 1 small chorizo, diced 1 red onion, chopped 4 garlic cloves, crushed 2 chillies, sliced	Heat a little oil in a wok and sauté until tender.
1 kilo mussels, scrubbed & de-bearded (see below) 1 cup dry white wine	Add, cover, and remove mussels as they open, discarding any that don't.
chopped fresh Italian (flat leaf) parsley	Pour all the juices over the top and sprinkle with parsley. Serves 2

'To prepare mussels, scrub with a stiff brush first then "de-beard" by grasping the string-like substance coming out of the shell and running it towards the hinge before pulling it off. And if any are already open before you cook them, give them a tap – if they don't close, discard them as they are dead.'

Homard à la Parisienne
(Cheese Gratinéed Lobster in Mustard Cream)

2 x 1.2 kilos lobsters, cooked	Cut in half. Take out meat and remove intestinal tract. Put lobster 'mustard' and tail shells aside. Cut lobster flesh into largish chunks, cover and set aside.
3 cups dry white wine 2 cups water 1 onion, sliced 1 medium carrot, diced coarsely 1 celery stalk, diced coarsely 6 whole black peppercorns a few sprigs of fresh parsley 1 bay leaf	Put in a large pot along with lobster heads. Bring to simmer and cook for 20 minutes.
4 tbsp butter 1 cup sliced button mushrooms 3 tbsp plain flour	Melt butter in a heavy-bottomed pot and sauté mushrooms until tender. Then add flour, mix well and cook over low heat for a few minutes.
1 cup thickened cream sea salt & freshly ground pepper Dijon mustard fresh lemon juice	Strain lobster stock into mushroom mixture and whisk well. Add cream, lobster 'mustard', seasoning and Dijon mustard to taste. Simmer and reduce to a sauce consistency. Flavour to taste with a little lemon juice.
grated tasty cheese	Preheat overhead grill. Add lobster to sauce and simmer very gently to heat. Mound into tail shells, top with cheese and cook under preheated grill until browned.

Serves 4

'On one of the earliest Tolarno menus, Lobster Parisienne was available for the princely sum of $2.30 – wouldn't that be nice?'

Bouillabaisse de Crabe

(Blue Swimmer Crabs in the Bouillabaisse Style)

4 blue swimmer crabs	Preheat oven to highest degree. Prepare crabs by lifting top shell away from body. Clean body by running under cold water. Cut crabs into quarters in a cross pattern. Then blanch 2 top shells in boiling water to use as a garnish.
olive oil 2 leeks, white part only, finely sliced 2 chillies, finely sliced 1 small fennel bulb, cleaned, cored & finely sliced 1 onion, finely sliced 3 garlic cloves, crushed	In a very large frying pan that can go in the oven, heat oil and sauté vegetables.
4 roma tomatoes, cored & quartered ½ cup fresh tomato puree 5 strands saffron 1 cup fish stock, bought (low salt) or homemade (page 255) a good slurp of Pernod	Add and cook for 15 minutes, adding more stock if needed. Then add crabs, toss well and cook in oven for 7–10 minutes until crabs are cooked. Put in deep bowls and top with blanched shells.
8 slices baguette, toasted or baked Aïoli (page 256) chopped fresh parsley	Serve with croutons and aïoli on the side with a sprinkling of parsley on top. Serves 2

'I have an allergy to crustaceans and suffer a severe reaction even when they're being cooked in the kitchen. After our marriage broke up, Ruth Allen, for a (thankfully) brief period took great delight in encouraging customers to order the bouillabaisse of crab.'

Les Crêpes aux Fruits de Mer
(Cheese Gratinéed Seafood Crepes)

2 large eggs 180 ml milk a pinch of sugar a pinch of sea salt 145 gm plain flour	Preheat overhead grill. To make crepes, whisk eggs, milk, sugar and salt. Then add flour and whisk until smooth (batter should be consistency of heavy cream). Set aside for 30 minutes.
a good knob of butter	Melt butter in a crepe pan and whisk into batter. Make 8 crepes a little thicker than usual by spooning a layer of batter into pan and cooking until browned on both sides. Repeat process until you have 8 crepes. When finished cover and set aside.
unsalted butter 200 gm skinless, boneless salmon, cubed 10 green prawns, peeled, deveined & chopped into largish pieces 8 fresh scallops, cleaned & halved	Heat a little butter in a pan, add seafood and toss for a minute or two.
16 oysters, freshly shucked grated tasty cheese thickened cream	Place a crepe in a large rectangular ovenproof dish. Scatter with seafood mix, then 2 oysters. Top with a generous amount of cheese and a good sprinkling of cream. Roll up and push to one end of gratin dish. Repeat process until all crepes are filled. Sprinkle cheese over top, sprinkle generously with cream and grill until golden and bubbling.

Serves 4

'Tolarno used to serve this in individual Le Creuset dishes. And a seafood crepe is not a way to use up all those leftover bits and pieces of seafood. Or those bloody awful marinara mixes or seafood fillers that the supermarkets are so keen on.'

Crevettes à l'Ail
(Garlic Prawns)

¼ cup olive oil 6 garlic cloves, finely chopped 1 kilo medium-sized green prawns, in the shell	Heat oil in a large pan. Add garlic and prawns in one layer. Cook, turning regularly, until prawns are bright pink all over and firm when squeezed (be careful not to burn garlic).
2 heaped tbsp butter 2 tbsp chopped fresh Italian (flat leaf) parsley juice of 1 lemon freshly ground pepper	Add, toss well and when butter is melted and incorporated, place the lot in bowls.
baguette	Serve with finger bowls, plenty of napkins and crusty bread to soak up juices. (Obviously prawns need to cool a bit before they can be shelled.) serves 2–4

'If you must, you can peel the prawns, but they will always be juicier and sweeter (and hard to peel) when cooked in the shells.'

Quenelles de Langouste aux Épinards et Sauce Rouge
(Lobster & Spinach Quenelles with Lobster Sauce)

2 cups milk 100 gm soft unsalted butter 600 gm plain flour, sifted	Place milk in a heavy-bottomed pot and bring to the boil. Add butter and flour and beat vigorously with a wooden spoon. When thick, turn down heat to very low and stir constantly to dry the 'panade'. Remove from heat and leave in a cool spot.
400 gm lobster meat 100 gm cooked spinach 4 tsp sea salt freshly ground pepper 2 tbsp finely chopped fresh coriander	Pound using a mortar and pestle (or whiz in a processor). When a smooth paste is formed, pass through a fine sieve. Return to mortar or processor bowl.
3 egg whites	Work whites in well, then mix in panade thoroughly.
12 eggs 400 gm soft unsalted butter	Add eggs, mix in well and when smooth, mix in butter. Chill mousse until firm.
lobster shells, crushed 1 carrot, chopped 1 onion, chopped 2 celery stalks, chopped 1 bay leaf	Preheat oven to 220°C. Put in a baking tray and cook in oven for about 20 minutes, stirring occasionally. Remove.
2 tbsp tomato paste 1 ½ tbsp brandy 2 litres fish stock, bought (low salt) or homemade (page 255) 2 cups thickened cream sea salt & freshly ground pepper	Add tomato paste and sauté in tray over moderate heat for 5 minutes then deglaze with a good splash of brandy. Add stock and simmer over low heat for 1 hour or until reduced by half. Strain through a fine sieve, add cream and seasoning along with 1 ½ tablespoons brandy. Cook for another 10 minutes over low heat.

50 gm soft unsalted butter 80 gm plain flour	Mix together then gradually whisk into sauce until thickened. Boil for about 5 minutes then strain through a fine sieve.
5 litres salted water	Shape mousse into quenelles using 2 tablespoons. Poach in hot, not boiling, salted water, for about 15 minutes until they resist slightly when pressed. Drain well on kitchen paper towels.
freshly grated parmesan fresh breadcrumbs 4 poached yabbies a few sprigs of fresh dill	Preheat oven to 220°C. Put quenelles in an ovenproof dish, generously coat with sauce and sprinkle over cheese and crumbs. Bake for 10 minutes and serve garnished with yabbies and dill. Serves 10

'Demonstrating how intricate some of the dishes were during the Massoni era, this recipe from the Tolarno menu circa 1985, is by chef Louis Ercout.'

Roasted Moreton Bay Bugs with Beurre Maître d'Hôtel

125 gm soft unsalted butter 2 garlic cloves, crushed 2 tbsp chopped fresh parsley juice of ½ lemon	Preheat oven to 200°C. Mix together until well blended. Put in a piping bag.
8 Moreton Bay bugs	Cut in half lengthways and clean. Pipe butter on top of meat and refrigerate for at least 30 minutes. Then put on a baking tray and cook in oven for about 15–20 minutes (check if cooked by making a small cut).
2 good handfuls mixed lettuce leaves balsamic vinegar olive oil	Place bugs on 4 plates and pour juices over the top. Dress lettuce leaves with vinegar and oil and mound alongside.

Serves 4

'The butter setting on top means that the bug meat firms and begins to cook before the butter melts over it.'

John Dory with Lemon & Caper Butter

plain flour sea salt & freshly ground pepper 1 x John Dory, fins removed	Mix together flour, salt and pepper and lightly dust fish. Shake off any excess.
olive oil a good knob of butter	Heat enough oil and butter to just cover base of a pan large enough to hold fish comfortably. Slip in fish and cook on both sides over moderate heat until golden. To check when ready, make small cut behind the head. Remove and keep warm.
another good knob or two of butter juice of ½ lemon 1 tbsp drained & chopped capers 1 tbsp chopped fresh Italian (flat leaf) parsley	Add to pan and, when lightly brown and foaming, pour over fish. Serves 1

'If you must, you can remove the head. And keep in mind that fish continues to cook once removed from the heat source, so keep it a little under, please.'

Saumon Grillé et Sauce Vierge
(Crispy Skinned Salmon with a Tomato, Fresh Herb & Lemon Oil)

olive oil
4 x 180 gm boned salmon steaks, with skin
24–30 baby green beans, topped & tailed

Preheat overhead grill.
Heat a little oil in a pan and sear salmon, flesh-side down. Then turn over and cook under grill, turning once or twice, and watching carefully to ensure that skin is crisp, not burnt. To check if ready, make a small cut – salmon should be opaque in centre, not cooked right through. When almost ready, blanch beans in a large pot of lightly salted rapidly boiling water. Drain well and divide among 4 plates. Top with salmon.

1 punnet cherry tomatoes, cut lengthways into 4 or 8
1 cup extra virgin olive oil
3 tbsp fresh lemon juice
sea salt & freshly ground pepper
3 tbsp chopped fresh herbs – a mixture of parsley, chervil & chives

Combine in a small pot and bring just to simmer. Ladle over salmon.

Serves 4

Fish 'n' Chips

1 cup freshly opened lager ½ cup cold water a good pinch of sea salt 1 tsp baking powder 1 ½–2 cups self-raising flour	Make batter by putting lager, water and salt in a large bowl. Mix baking powder into flour and add to liquid, little by little, whisking continually. Enough flour has been added when the batter coats your finger lightly.
6–8 cups vegetable oil chips, either bought or homemade (page 211) sea salt	Put oil in a large deep-sided pot and heat to 190°C. Fry chips until golden, then drain well on kitchen paper towels and sprinkle with sea salt. Keep hot in a low oven.
8 x 80 gm pieces of boneless, skinless fish (favourites include blue eye, whiting, flathead & snapper) Tartare Sauce (page 256) lemon wedges	Bring oil back to 190°C. Then, without overcrowding, dip fish in batter, put carefully in hot oil and fry until golden. Drain on kitchen paper towels. Sprinkle with salt and serve with chips, tartare and lemon wedges on the side. Serves 4

'A deep-frying thermometer is almost essential.'

Truite aux Amandes
(Trout with Almonds)

olive oil a good knob of butter	In a pan large enough to hold both fish, heat oil and butter to cover base.
plain flour 2 plate sized fresh trout sea salt & freshly ground pepper	Lightly flour trout and season, then pan-fry over moderate heat until golden. To check when ready, make a small cut behind head. Remove fish to serving plates.
2 good knobs of butter 2 heaped tbsp slivered almonds	Add and cook gently until almonds are golden.
2 good squeezes of fresh lemon juice 1 heaped tbsp chopped fresh parsley	Add, mix and pour over fish. Serves 2

'During the sixties and even the early seventies, it was difficult, if not impossible, to buy fresh fish. (I remember once asking a waiter during this period whether the fish was fresh. His reply: "Absolutely – it's fresh frozen.") Trout was an exception to this rule as trout farms were springing up everywhere and the fish was not only fresh but relatively inexpensive. Trout with Almonds was a popular menu item during the Mora years.'

Thon Marmitako

(Tuna with a Spiced Tomato, Capsicum & Potato Stew)

olive oil 1 large red onion, cut into thin wedges 1 large red capsicum, cored, seeded & cut into chunks 1 large yellow capsicum, cored, seeded & cut into chunks 1 large green capsicum, cored, seeded & cut into chunks 3 garlic cloves, crushed 3 chillies, sliced	Heat a little oil in a large deep-sided pan and sauté until tender.
½ cup dry white wine	Add and reduce by half.
2 x 400 gm cans diced tomatoes, drained a little 1–2 cups fish or vegetable stock, bought (low salt) or homemade (page 255) 8 baby potatoes, peeled & halved or quartered sea salt & freshly ground pepper	Add and simmer until potatoes are tender, adding more stock as needed.
1 x 600 gm piece of tuna, cleaned of bloodline 12 fresh basil leaves, torn	Cut tuna into 1 ½–2 cm cubes. Add to sauce along with basil and mix well. Cook for 4 or so minutes, then serve. Serves 4

'A specialty of France's Basque region where they love spicy food.'

Snapper with Pistou Mash, Parmesan & Brown Butter

4 x 180 gm boneless, skinless snapper fillets juice of ½ lemon olive oil sea salt & freshly ground pepper	Preheat overhead grill. Put snapper on a baking tray and toss with lemon juice, a good slurp of oil and seasoning. Set aside.
6 large potatoes, peeled & quartered	Boil in salted water until tender. Drain well and return to pot.
¼–½ cup milk sea salt & freshly ground pepper	Put pot back on heat, add ¼ cup milk and when bubbling, mash, adding more milk if needed. Check seasoning and add if needed.
Basil Pistou (page 257)	Add to taste and mound onto 4 plates.
100 gm unsalted butter freshly shaved parmesan	When potatoes are almost ready, grill snapper, turning once, until just opaque in the centre. Place on mash. Put butter in a pan and, when lightly brown, pour over snapper. Top with parmesan shavings.

Serves 4

Filet de Merlan Meunière
(Whiting Fillets with Lemon Butter)

olive oil a good knob of butter	Heat a thin layer of oil and butter in a large pan until sizzling.
plain flour 8 boneless, skinless whiting fillets sea salt & freshly ground pepper	Flour fish lightly and season. Fry until golden brown in 2 or 3 lots, adding a little more oil and butter if needed. Remove and put on 4 plates.
4 tbsp butter a good squeeze of fresh lemon juice 1 heaped tbsp chopped fresh parsley	Add to pan and when lightly browned, pour over fish.
lemon wedges	Serve with lemon wedges on the side and a simple salad or green vegetables.

Serves 4

'Another true bistro classic, this featured on the Tolarno menus throughout the various eras. And, to this day, it is still about the best way to cook spotlessly fresh whiting (or in fact, any delicate fish fillets).'

Brochettes d'Agneau
Carré d'Agneau Persillé
Navarin d'Agneau Printanier
Gigot d'Agneau Rôti à la Provençale
Escalopes de Veau au Citron
Hachis Parmentier
Parmesan-crumbed Veal with Dubonnet & Orange
Blanquette de Veau à l'Ancienne
Jarret de Veau à la Ménagère
Kangaroo with Barley & Pumpkin Pilaf and a Black Pepper & Lemon-spiked Sauce
Boudin Noir aux Pommes
Cervelles d'Agneau Grenobloise
Ragoût de Lucullus
Rognons d'Agneau à la Diable
Langue de Boeuf Grillée avec Sauce Rémoulade
Tripes à la Lyonnaise

LAMB, VEAL
and Bits & Pieces

'There is one mistake we nearly all make when first attempting French cookery. We make it too complicated. A galaxy of seasonings, oceans of wine and cream, thick sauces and a mass of garnishes are alien to the whole spirit of French cookery.'

Elizabeth David
French Provincial Cooking, 1960

Brochettes d'Agneau

(Lamb & Lambs' Kidneys on Skewers)

2 lamb backstraps (boned, trimmed loin)	Cut into 2 cm thick slices.
¼ cup olive oil 2 garlic cloves, crushed 1 heaped tsp fresh rosemary needles sea salt & freshly ground pepper	Whisk in a bowl, add lamb and refrigerate for at least 3 hours, tossing every now and then.
4 lambs' kidneys, cleaned, cored & quartered 1 red capsicum, cored, seeded & cut into pieces of a similar size to lamb 1 red onion, peeled & cut to similar size 12 fresh bay leaves	Preheat ridged grill or BBQ. Thread lamb and kidneys onto 4 large metal skewers, interspersing with capsicum, onion and bay leaves.
olive oil spray 1–2 lemons, halved	Lightly oil grill and cook skewers to desired degree, brushing with marinade and squeezing with lemon as you do so.
Tomates à la Provençale (page 208)	Serve brochettes with the tomatoes. Serves 4

'This was one of my favourites at Tolarno Two–Brochettes, which was the Massonis' casual eatery on the right side of the Tolarno corridor (which eventually turned into Le Bar during the Hewitson–Allen reign).'

Carré d'Agneau Persillé
(Rack of Lamb with Garlic & Herb Crumbs)

100 gm fresh breadcrumbs, made from 2-day-old sourdough bread 2 large garlic cloves, crushed 3 tbsp chopped fresh parsley 75 gm unsalted butter, melted	Mix together, adding more crumbs if too liquid.
4 x 5-point lamb racks, trimmed of all fat & sinew Dijon mustard	Paint meat lightly with mustard and press crumbs firmly on top. Refrigerate for at least 2 hours.
olive oil spray	Preheat oven to 200°C. Put racks in baking tray, spray with oil and cook in oven to the desired degree (about 10–15 minutes for medium–rare). Rest for 5 minutes.
Ratatouille Niçoise (page 66)	Cut into cutlets and serve on a bed of ratatouille with any juices on top.

Serves 4

Navarin d'Agneau Printanier
(Braised Lamb with Vegetables)

olive oil 1 kilo lean, cubed lamb	Heat oil in a large heavy-bottomed pot and seal lamb until well coloured in 2 or 3 lots, reheating oil between each lot. Set aside.
1 large onion, chopped 3 garlic cloves, crushed 2 medium carrots, peeled & cut into thickish slices 2 celery stalks, diced	Wipe out pan, add new oil, heat and sauté until tender and lightly coloured.
2 heaped tbsp plain flour	Add, mix well and cook over low heat for 5 minutes, stirring regularly.
1 litre beef stock, bought (low salt) or homemade (page 254) 1 x 400 gm can diced tomatoes, drained a little 2 bay leaves 2 sprigs fresh thyme sea salt & freshly ground pepper	Add and mix well. Bring to the boil, add lamb and gently simmer for 1 hour, adding more stock if needed.
12 baby turnips, peeled 12 baby potatoes, peeled 4 small leeks, washed well & cut in 3 crossways	Add and cook for another 30 minutes or until both meat and vegetables are very tender.
1 cup frozen peas	Add for last 10 minutes.

Serves 6

Gigot d'Agneau Rôti à la Provençale
(Roast Leg of Lamb with the Flavours of Provence)

1 leg of lamb, trimmed of excess fat sea salt & freshly ground pepper	Preheat oven to 220°C. Season well.
12 small sprigs fresh rosemary 3 garlic cloves, thinly sliced 6 anchovies, halved olive oil spray ½ lemon	Make 12 cuts in lamb. Poke a sliver or two of garlic, a rosemary sprig and half an anchovy into each then spray with oil and squeeze lemon juice over.
chicken stock, bought (low salt) or homemade (page 254)	Put lamb in roasting tray and add a slurp of stock. Roast for about 1–1 ¼ hours, basting and adding slurps of stock every now and then. (To check when ready, push a thin knife blade in – the juices should have a pink tinge and blade should be hot to the touch.) Remove lamb from tray and rest on a plate, loosely covered with foil, for 15 minutes. Then, add more stock to roasting tray and boil to reduce, scraping up any brown bits.
Gratin Dauphinois (page 212)	Carve lamb and serve with strained juices and gratin on the side. Serves 8–10

'For Sunday lunch during the Massoni era, there was often a wonderful garlic scented gigot of lamb served simply with a creamy potato gratin and some pan juices – delicious.'

Escalopes de Veau au Citron
(Sautéed Veal with Lemon)

4 x 120 gm veal escalopes (or scaloppine as they are often called)	Batten out lightly to an even thickness.
plain flour sea salt & freshly ground pepper	Flour lightly and season.
olive oil a good knob of butter	Heat oil and butter in a large heavy-bottomed pan until foaming. Then add veal, 2 at a time, and seal on each side. Remove.
12 fresh sage leaves ½ cup dry white wine grated rind & juice of 1 lemon ½ cup thickened cream sea salt & freshly ground pepper	Add sage, cook for a few minutes, then add wine. Reduce by half, then add lemon and cream. Bring to the boil, return veal and any juices and cook very gently until sauce has thickened, turning once or twice. Check seasoning.
40 small green beans, topped & tailed chopped fresh parsley	Blanch in plenty of salted, boiling water. Put on plates, top with veal and sauce. Sprinkle with parsley.

Serves 4

'I had a wife who, every time we visited Tolarno during the days of Leon and Vivienne, ordered this dish. After demonstrating such a lack of adventure, it's not surprising the marriage didn't last.'

Hachis Parmentier
(Shepherd's Pie)

vegetable oil 1 large carrot, peeled & diced 3 rindless bacon rashers, diced 1 onion, finely chopped 2 celery stalks, diced	Preheat oven to 220°C. Heat oil in a large heavy-bottomed pot. Add and sauté gently for 5 minutes.
750 gm lean minced lamb (or beef)	Turn up heat, add and stir, mashing mince as you do so, until mince changes colour.
½ cup dry white wine 1 cup beef stock, bought (low salt) or homemade (page 254) ½ + cup canned tomato puree 3 tbsp tomato chutney sea salt & freshly ground pepper 2 bay leaves	Add with the half-cup of tomato puree. Mix very well, turn down heat and simmer for 30 minutes until thick and fragrant, adding more puree if needed. Discard bay leaves and put in large ovenproof dish.
Creamy Mash (page 209) grated tasty cheese freshly grated parmesan	Spread mash over top and sprinkle generously with both cheeses. Cook in oven until golden and bubbling. Serves 8–10

'This started life as Hachis Parmentier during our French period but quickly turned into Shepherd's Pie. One of our most popular mains, even in summer, there were almost pickets in the street when I once decided to remove it from the menu – I didn't make that mistake again, no matter how hot it was.'

Parmesan-crumbed Veal with Dubonnet & Orange

600 gm veal fillet, trimmed of all fat & sinew	Cut into 4 equal lengths. Butterfly each piece by cutting through the middle, parallel to the bench, leaving one edge attached. Spread out and gently batten out with a meat mallet.
plain flour sea salt & freshly ground pepper 2 eggs ½ cup milk 1 cup breadcrumbs ½ cup freshly grated parmesan 2 tbsp chopped fresh parsley	In 3 separate bowls, put flour and seasonings; beaten eggs and milk; and crumbs mixed with parmesan and parsley. Dip veal first in flour, then into eggwash and then firmly into crumbs.
olive oil 2 tbsp finely chopped onion ½ cup Dubonnet ½ cup fresh orange juice 1 tbsp chopped fresh parsley 2 good knobs of butter	Heat oil in a pan and sauté onion until tender. Then add Dubonnet, orange juice and parsley and cook down until reduced by two-thirds. Add butter and cook until it melts.
olive oil	When sauce is almost ready, heat a layer of oil in a large non-stick pan and cook veal until golden brown in 2 or 3 lots. Drain well on kitchen paper towels and serve in a pool of sauce.

Serves 4

'Dubonnet is a French apéritif normally drunk over ice with a good squeeze of lemon.'

Blanquette de Veau à l'Ancienne
(White Veal Stew with Onions & Mushrooms)

1.25 kilos veal shoulder, trimmed well & cut into 3 cm cubes	Place in a pot, cover with cold water and bring to simmer. Simmer for 2 minutes. Drain and wash quickly under cold water. Wipe out pot.
5–6 cups chicken stock, bought (low salt) or homemade (page 254) 1 large onion, peeled & studded with 1 clove 1 large carrot, peeled & quartered 2 celery stalks, cut into lengths 3 sprigs fresh thyme 3 strips lemon rind, all pith removed 3 sprigs fresh parsley sea salt a good splash of dry vermouth	Return veal to pot and just cover with stock. Bring slowly to simmer, skimming any impurities. Then add rest of ingredients, cover, and simmer very gently for 45 minutes–1 hour until veal is tender. Strain, reserving stock, and removing veal. Discard vegetables.
24 small button mushrooms, wiped clean with a damp cloth 24 baby (pickling) onions, peeled ½ cup chicken stock, bought (low salt) or homemade (page 254)	When veal is almost ready, simmer gently until onions are fairly tender.
3 tbsp plain flour	Add and mix very well. Cook for another few minutes.
sea salt & freshly ground pepper fresh lemon juice	Add strained veal stock, bring to simmer and add seasoning and lemon juice to taste. Return veal and mix well. Simmer for 5 or so minutes.
3 large egg yolks ½ cup thickened cream 2 tbsp chopped fresh parsley	Whisk together, remove blanquette from heat and mix in well. Serve either on a bed of steamed rice or with any green vegetables alongside.

Serves 6

Jarret de Veau à la Menagère
(Home-style Veal Shanks)

olive oil plain flour sea salt & freshly ground pepper 6 veal shanks, French trimmed	Heat a layer of oil in a large heavy-bottomed pot. Flour and season shanks and cook until browned all over. Remove.
2 carrots, diced 1 large onion, finely chopped 4 celery stalks, diced 3 garlic cloves, crushed	Adding more oil if needed, add and sauté until tender.
1 ½ cups dry white wine	Add and reduce by two-thirds.
3 cups beef stock, bought (low salt) or homemade (page 254) 1 x 400 gm can diced tomatoes, drained a little sea salt & freshly ground pepper	Add and bring to the boil. Return shanks and bury in liquid. Cover and gently simmer for 1½ hours or so until shanks are very tender, adding more stock if needed. Season to taste.
chopped fresh Italian parsley	Serve with all the juices and vegetables over the top and a sprinkling of parsley.

Serves 6

'You can also, if you like, give these shanks a bit of an Italian feel by sprinkling with gremolata, which is made from finely chopped lemon and orange peel, garlic and parsley.'

Generous, hospitable and knowledgeable are the first words I would be inclined to apply to Leon and Vivienne Massoni, and also to David Gibson, Vivienne's son, when he joined the team. And it was these qualities which, to me at least, were the key to their huge success with Tolarno French Bistro.

One of their former kitchen staff members – *Age Good Food Guide* young chef of the year and a former Fleurie pastry chef, Emma Mackay, once provided me with a revealing insight into the extraordinary contribution Leon made to the team effort.

Without exception, Emma told me, Leon would visit the Tolarno kitchen before every meal service, would taste all the sauces and soups, and would also check the level and quality of the preparation.

Also, after donning a pair of white cotton gloves, he would meticulously weigh every steak, every portion of fish, and anything else he thought needed weighing. Just to be sure …

Vivienne's eye was as keen as Leon's. And later, David implemented a degree of computerisation hitherto unknown in the restaurant business, allowing Leon to reflect market cost variations by making those last-minute changes to menu prices for which he became famous.

In short, all three members of the Massoni team demonstrated a level of dedication and expertise, and of attention to detail, that ensured Tolarno's enduring appeal throughout the Massoni era.

Kangaroo with Barley & Pumpkin Pilaf and a Black Pepper & Lemon-spiked Sauce

olive oil 1 onion, chopped 3 garlic cloves, crushed	Heat a little oil in a large heavy-bottomed pot and sauté until tender.
2 tsp cracked black pepper 2 tsp cumin seeds 3 tsp paprika 2 cinnamon sticks, halved	Add and toss for a minute or so.
1.5 litres beef stock, bought (low salt) or homemade (page 254)	Add and reduce to a sauce consistency.
juice of 2 lemons ½ cup chopped fresh coriander	Add and cook for a couple of minutes.
½ butternut pumpkin, peeled, seeded & cubed olive oil	Preheat oven to 180°C. Put pumpkin in a roasting tray, sprinkle with oil and roast until very soft.
200 gm pearl barley 1 litre chicken stock, bought (low salt) or homemade (page 254)	Rinse barley under cold water. Drain well then cook in stock until tender.
sea salt & freshly ground pepper	Add pumpkin, season and keep warm (if too much liquid drain a little off).
olive oil spray 6–8 kangaroo fillets, trimmed of all fat & sinew sea salt & freshly ground pepper	Preheat ridged grill. Oil and season meat. Cook kangaroo over high heat to no more than medium–rare but crusty all over. Rest for 5 minutes. Mound pilaf on plates, top with sliced meat and a good spoonful or two of sauce.

Serves 6–8

Boudin Noir aux Pommes
(Black Pudding with Apples)

2–3 tbsp butter 2–3 tbsp sugar 3 Granny Smith apples, peeled, cored & cut into wedges chicken stock, bought (low salt) or homemade (page 254)	Melt butter and sugar in a large heavy-bottomed pan, add apples and cook gently, adding a little stock if caramelising too much. Cook until tender but still whole.
olive oil 3–4 black puddings	Heat oil in another pan, cut puddings into thick slices and cook in 2 or 3 lots until crispy.
Creamy Mash (page 209)	Serve just with apple or, if you like, on a bed of mash with the apples spooned over the top. Serves 4

'In similar vein to tripe, you either love or hate black pudding. But, as was the case with tripe, this was always very popular whenever it featured on Tolarno's menu.'

Cervelles d'Agneau Grenobloise
(Lambs' Brains with Brown Butter)

4–6 sets of lambs' brains juice of ½ lemon 1 sprig of fresh parsley ¼ onion, sliced a splash of white vinegar water	Soak brains for a few hours in cold water with a good squeeze of lemon juice. Drain and put in pot along with parsley, onion, vinegar and water to cover. Bring to the boil, turn off and cool in the water. Then drain well and separate each set of brains into two, removing any membrane.
4 cornichons (baby gherkins), diced 2 lemons, segmented 2 tbsp drained & chopped capers 2 tbsp chopped fresh parsley	Mix together and set aside.
plain flour olive oil unsalted butter	Dust brains with flour and heat a layer of oil in a large heavy-bottomed pan. Cook brains until golden on all sides. Place on plates. Add a few good dollops of butter and lemon mixture to pan and cook until foaming. Pour over brains. Serves 4

Ragoût de Lucullus
(Brain, Yabbie & Sweetbread Stew)

1 pair of sweetbreads	Put in cold water and soak for 3 hours, changing water at least 3 or 4 times.
2 calves' brains 1 tbsp white wine vinegar	In another bowl, soak brains in a similar manner, adding vinegar for last hour.
sea salt & freshly ground pepper vegetable oil	Drain both and remove and discard connective tissues and membranes. Dry and season. Heat oil in a large heavy-bottomed pan and cook until lightly browned.
½ cup hot beef stock, bought (low salt) or homemade (page 254)	Put in a bowl. Slice brains and sweetbreads into 1-cm pieces, then dice and add. Set aside.
2 small carrots, peeled 2 celery stalks 2 small leeks, washed well 2 turnips, peeled 1 ½ cups beef stock, bought (low salt) or homemade (page 254)	Cut the vegetables into julienne strips, then boil in the stock until tender. Drain, reserving stock and add vegetables to brains and sweetbreads.
½ cup French vermouth ¼ cup minced red (French) shallots 1 tbsp chopped fresh tarragon extra beef stock 1 cup crème fraiche sea salt & freshly ground pepper	At same time, put vermouth, shallots and tarragon in another pan and reduce by half. Top up reserved stock with extra beef stock to 2 ½ cups, add to vermouth mix and reduce by half. Add crème fraiche and, once again, reduce by half then strain. Return to pan.
12 yabbie tails, shelled & deveined	Add and gently warm. Then drain brains, sweetbread, and vegetables and add. Serve in large flat soup bowls. Serves 4

'A recipe from Tolarno circa 1982.'

Rognons d'Agneau à la Diable
(Devilled Lambs' Kidneys)

12-16 lambs' kidneys	Remove membrane, cut in half lengthways and, with a sharp knife or kitchen scissors, cut out the core. Then cut each half into 2 or 3 pieces.
olive oil	Heat in a pan and, in 2 or 3 lots, quickly seal kidneys. Remove and set aside.
½ medium onion, finely chopped 2 garlic cloves, crushed	Adding a little more oil if necessary, sauté until tender.
½ cup chicken stock, bought (low salt) or homemade (page 254) ⅓ cup thickened cream 1 heaped tsp Dijon mustard a good splash of Worcestershire sauce a good splash or two of Tabasco 1 tbsp chopped fresh parsley	Add, bring to the boil and reduce by one-third. Then return kidneys and cook very, very gently for 2–3 minutes.
4 thick slices sourdough bread chopped fresh parsley	Grill or toast sourdough, put on plates and top with kidneys. Sprinkle with parsley. Serves 4

'The most important thing when cooking kidneys – don't overcook, they should still be pink in the centre.'

Langue de Boeuf Grillée avec Sauce Rémoulade
(Ox Tongue with Herb Mayonnaise)

2 ox tongues, brined for 24 hours 6 sprigs fresh parsley 1 large celery stalk, sliced 1 large carrot, peeled & sliced 1 medium onion, sliced 2 garlic cloves, crushed 1 tsp whole black peppercorns	Put in a large heavy-bottomed pot and cover with water. Bring to the boil and simmer for 1–1 ½ hours or until tongue tips are tender when squeezed between your fingers. Remove and cool. When cooking, weigh tongues down with a plate to keep under liquid.
1 tsp chopped fresh tarragon 1 tsp chopped fresh oregano 1 tsp chopped fresh thyme 2 tbsp chopped fresh parsley 1 garlic clove, crushed 4 anchovies, chopped 1 tbsp drained & chopped capers 1 tbsp red onion, finely chopped	Combine in a bowl.
1 cup Aïoli (page 256) 1 extra heaped tsp Dijon mustard a splash of tarragon vinegar	Add and fold very carefully into herb mixture.
	Preheat ridged grill or BBQ. Peel tongue and cut into thick slices. Grill on both sides then serve with sauce flicked over the top (and a little of the cooking liquid if you like). Serves 6–8

Tripes à la Lyonnaise
(Tripe & Onions in the Style of Lyon)

1 kilo pre-cooked honeycomb tripe	Cut into small sticks approximately 5 mm thick and 8–10 cm long.
3 tbsp olive oil 1 good knob butter 3 onions, finely sliced 1 tsp sugar	Heat oil and butter in a large heavy-bottomed pan to smoking. Add onions and sugar and cook until golden, stirring frequently.
4 tbsp olive oil 1 good knob of butter sea salt & freshly ground pepper a good splash or two of red wine vinegar chopped fresh Italian (flat leaf) parsley	Heat oil and butter in another pan until smoking and add tripe. Season and cook until crispy and well coloured. Then add to onions and mix well, cooking for a few minutes. Add vinegar and parsley. Cook briefly and serve very hot.

Serves 6–8

'When I first took over Tolarno this was one of my French classics on the first menu. Surprisingly, it sold well – maybe it's because tripe is rarely cooked at home anymore.'

The HEWITSON-ALLEN Years

*L*oose lips, as they say during world wars and lesser skirmishes, sink ships. And if the restaurateur who in the early 1990s was formulating plans for St Kilda's iconic Tolarno French Bistro had kept that in mind on the night he dined in Iain 'Huey' Hewitson's Memories of the Mediterranean restaurant in Melbourne's Exhibition Street, things may have turned out quite differently. But let Huey explain ...

'I was in Memories one night when I ran into someone who told me, quite casually, that he was planning to buy Tolarno, the bistro in St Kilda. I congratulated him, told him how much I loved the place and, also, how much I loved the Mirka Mora murals around the walls,' says Huey.

'He then told me, proudly, that I could forget about the murals because the first thing he was going to do when he took possession was to get rid of them. To paint over them. Whatever. I was speechless, which is not something that happens to me every night of the week.'

And so it came to pass that Huey, after a sleepless night because of his concerns for the wellbeing of artwork that had given new direction to the dining traditions of Melbourne, artwork he loved dearly, called the agent involved. He learned that despite the claims of his acquaintance, the lease for Tolarno French Bistro was still up for grabs. Huey made an offer, it was accepted and, yet again, the Mirka Mora murals had worked their magic.

And so it came to pass that in 1991, through an arrangement finalised with the sheriff due to the financial discomforts being experienced by the vendors, Huey, in partnership with his former wife, Sandra, and a friend, Tony Gowing, from a well-known Melbourne restaurant family, signed a lease that delivered them Tolarno French Bistro in 42 Fitzroy Street, St Kilda. Just like that. The Mirka Mora murals were, once again, in the safest of hands.

'At that point in my life, I needed a restaurant about as urgently as I needed a hole in the head,' says Huey. 'Memories was doing really well and I had just started working on television in *Healthy, Wealthy & Wise*, and it was looking like that was going to do pretty well, also. But there are some things in life that you just have to do, no matter what. It was Mirka's murals that sold me – no doubt about it. I loved them. I knew they had to be saved. And that was the end of that.'

Or rather, that was the beginning of that. Because after a few sad, misguided years in the dark after the glittering Massoni era, Tolarno French Bistro was once again in the hands of an inspired, innovative restaurateur who understood it, cared about it, and was about to bring it kicking, struggling, but breathing easily through a challenging decade, and beyond.

Iain Hewitson is, in every sense of the word, formidable. He is an outspoken, articulate, sensibly proportioned Kiwi with uncanny kitchen skills that have been acquired the hard way. He is probably as widely read on culinary matters as any chef alive. And he is, with some justification, at least as opinionated. He has a persona that works as well on television as Mirka Mora's murals work on walls, as his daily cooking programs – which number rather more than 1000 and seem to have been around for as long as TV test patterns – demonstrate. And he is that most unusual of individuals: a ferocious romantic, a man with an immense heart and a short fuse. It is entirely reasonable to suggest, therefore, that there is nobody, anywhere, quite like Huey. Least of all in St Kilda's Fitzroy Street.

Huey suffers fools with the same sort of enthusiasm he displays for careless kitchen staff, clueless waiters or any rugby fan not in awe of the All Blacks. But at the same time, he has a sentimental streak and a keen sense of history, and these worked in tandem to bring about his ownership of Tolarno Bistro. (It was Huey, incidentally, who dropped the 'F' word from the original name of the place – not due to any insensitivity to the past on his part, but because the frightful Frogs had decided to explode nuclear devices in the Pacific. Huey, not unreasonably, disapproved.)

'The original Tolarno French Bistro was the first restaurant I visited when I first came to Australia in the late 1960s. I knew nothing about it, had never even heard of it

in fact, but I was a cookbook collector, even then, and one day I went to the Hill of Content bookshop in Bourke Street to collect something or other,' says Huey. 'I started talking to somebody there, a foodie, who clearly knew his stuff. He told me his favourite restaurant in Melbourne was Tolarno, and I decided to go there immediately. And I loved everything about the place.

'I can still remember walking through the door and looking round, and seeing the painted walls. And I can still remember what I ate. I started with mussels, a dish you very seldom saw on menus in those days. And I had a steak with café de Paris butter and ratatouille and, to finish, a crème caramel, which was quite beautiful.

'I ate there several times, always at Sunday lunch as I was working by then, and that was my only free day. And it was always great – good food, and a great little place with plenty of atmosphere. It was alive. I remember that on Sundays, we had to be there by 2 pm because that's when they closed the kitchen. And we always made it.'

In the late 1960s, Huey left Australia and set off to conquer the world. Or, at least, some of it. He spent time in the United Kingdom and in France before returning to New Zealand to open a restaurant. But he still remembered the murals and those St Kilda mussels and, especially, that crème caramel. And so, in 1974, he returned to Melbourne.

Huey's return had an effect on the local restaurant scene not unlike the impact World War II had on the development of the fighter plane. After attracting attention, improbably, at the Lemon Tree, a pub in Carlton, he moved through a series of seminal establishments – Clichy, Fleurie, Champagne Charlie's, and the outrageously successful Last Aussie Fish Cafs which, after the success of the South Melbourne prototype, he also opened elsewhere in the country. Until, finally, he settled back into Melbourne and opened Memories of the Mediterranean in Rockman's Regency Hotel in Exhibition Street.

And soon Huey returned as a paying customer to Tolarno French Bistro. He became a regular, and remained a loyal supporter of the Sunday lunches served there. At that stage Georges Mora was still in charge although, in all honesty, he was beginning to lose interest: at least some of the blush had gone from the rose. But Huey still loved the place. And enjoyed the bistro food. And was still entranced, of course, by Mirka's marvellous murals.

Change was in the wind, however. And soon Georges withdrew to his art business, retaining his gallery in the Tolarno building, and Leon Massoni took over the bistro, as well as the Pancake Zoo.

The Tolarno French Bistro regulars, including Huey, were troubled at the thought of a new broom. And their thoughts about the new owners, considered now, shines an interesting light on Huey's own involvement with Tolarno, years later:

'When Leon and Vivienne Massoni took over, there was some disquiet,' says Huey. 'How could they possibly replace Georges and Mirka when they weren't even French? But within a very short time, we were won over: we realised that they were consummate restaurateurs.'

Which they were. But little did Huey realise, at the time, that as the Tolarno tale unfolded, there would be room for at least

one more consummate restaurateur to have his way with the place. A Kiwi, in fact. Called Iain Hewitson.

When Huey and his partners signed the lease, the idea was for Tony to run the place with Huey, who lived nearby, creating the menu, schooling the kitchen brigade, and dropping by occasionally to ensure that all was well. But for a restaurateur as instinctive as Huey, 'occasionally' was never going to work: he started to spend more and more time at Tolarno.

Sandra, the third partner, dropped out quite soon after the business had been established and Huey bought her share. And it was Sandra, also, who introduced Huey to a very capable restaurant manager called Ruth Allen, who was soon running Memories for Huey, and spending her remaining spare time in his company. They became a couple and moved into a flat they had created on the ground floor of the Tolarno building.

Ruth continued to run Memories until the day she realised she was urgently in need of a holiday. She decided to take a couple of months off. But sadly for Ruth, all was not well at Tolarno, and Huey had a fresh challenge for her.

'I was living in Tolarno with Iain, but I had no intention of ever working there,' says Ruth. 'But suddenly, Iain told me he needed help. Tony also was leaving the business and Iain was desperate. He agreed that when I finished at Memories I could take two days off. Then, he would need me at Tolarno – but only for a few days here, and a few days there. Or so he said. In reality, I never left Tolarno. I am still here.'

Through something close to natural selection, Huey finally owned the restaurant he wanted, and it was being run by the team he wanted, which included himself. But getting there had been costly: there was much ground to be made up before Huey and Ruth were in the clear, and only hard work, passion and ingenuity were going to get them there.

Huey's original idea had been simply to restore Tolarno Bistro to its former glory – to turn it back into the restaurant with which he had fallen in love, all those years ago. But the patrons, to his dismay, had other ideas.

'We did very little to the inside of the restaurant: we improved the lighting, removed the curtains and put a ledge behind the banquettes which had been there since Georges' day, and which had been regarded as pretty revolutionary when they were installed,' says Huey.

'As far as the food was concerned, I thought I would simply take things back to the way they were and the old customers would flow back. But strange as it may seem now with a resurgence in French bistro food under way, it quickly became apparent that, in the early 1990s, the authentic stuff that was Tolarno's signature was dead and buried.

'My first menus, which concentrated on such things as pissaladière, steak au poivre and the like, simply didn't prove as popular as I had expected. My business plan, based upon a return to the good old days, had to be abandoned and, instead, I made the menu far more eclectic.

'We developed the former Brochettes area into Le Bar, and that took off almost immediately, as did the food we served there. And if there was one dish that marked the final acceptance of Tolarno Bistro as a place that St Kilda could not live without, it was the Tolarno Burger. It was a huge hit from the day it appeared, as were the polenta chips and the crumbed mushrooms. They are still outrageously popular.

'But when a Melbourne newspaper declared the Tolarno Burger to be Australia's best and people poured into the bistro, demanding burgers, I became quite depressed about the bloody thing. I even threatened, in my darker moments, to abandon the Tolarno name altogether and rename the entire place Huey's Burger Bar. And, who knows...'

Huey did no such thing, however, which is fortunate. Because as Melbourne came to terms with the new Tolarno Bistro, they also came to appreciate Huey's 'new' bistro food. It exhibited the same attitude and adventure that had always been present in Tolarno food, but this was food for the 1990s. There was, for example, a tagine of duck confit, kangaroo in many guises, steak with sweet potato bubble and squeak, and even a Thai chicken curry which appeared after Huey had filmed a television special in Thailand, and which was quickly locked into the menu through the enthusiasm of regulars.

Tolarno Bistro, then, sported a menu which was no longer French, and had evolved out of circumstances which, according to every restaurateur (but one) worth his salt, are a recipe for disaster. The customers had spoken, the restaurateur had listened, and a business plan had been torn up and discarded. And as it began to work, Huey decided that there was no longer room for Memories of the Mediterranean in his full life, but there was room for a new wife. Her name was Ruth Allen.

'A unique thing about the people who come here is the St Kilda factor,' says Ruth. 'The managing director of a city firm can have a best mate who works as a waiter down the road, a shift worker, who has no money. And Tolarno Bistro, for some reason, provides common ground – a place where they can meet, and where they can eat and drink stylishly, but according to their own needs. The managing director can have one of the serious dishes from the menu, if he likes, while his mate can have a burger. One can drink great vintage wine while the other can choose a cleanskin. Your call. Friends with very different tastes and incomes still get together here.'

The democratic, mod-bohemian aspects of Tolarno Bistro suggest that under Huey, it is a place that has evolved more along the lines of the Mora model than the Massoni model. Is this how Huey sees it?

'Yes, absolutely,' he says. 'In Leon's day, this was one of Melbourne's elite restaurants – there is no doubt about that. But by the time we came along, a dozen or more places had passed it by. It was no longer a place that people went to on special occasions: it had returned to being a local place, a place for people to eat at in St Kilda. And once we understood, and accepted, that we had to create a place for regulars that was also attractive to others, we were on our way.'

But in the process, Huey learnt something: that the ferocity with which Tolarno regulars were prepared to shield their menu from interference, even from Huey, the man who created it, was both extraordinary and unique.

'I have never encountered anything like it,' says Huey. 'Once, I took the shepherd's pie off the menu and replaced it with a very stylish navarin of lamb pie. It was beautiful, and I absolutely love navarin of lamb. But we had a revolt on our hands; regulars threatened to establish a picket line, with signs, outside the restaurant unless I put the shepherd's pie back. Which I had to do.

'And in another rash moment, I decided to upgrade the burger by adding beetroot chutney and replacing the mustard with a mustard aioli. And not only did I get howls of protest about it, I even got abusive emails. Customers would never have dared to do that to Leon. I envy him ...'

Iain Hewitson – after fifteen fascinating, at times frustrating, but always enjoyable years at Tolarno Bistro – is a chef at the top of his game, and at the height of his celebrity. He is happily married – but to Ruth Krawat, not to Ruth Allen. And he is

genuinely besotted with married life, and with their daughter, Charlotte.

Also, he has satisfied another passion, another love of his life, by owning and operating the modest St Kilda bistro with which he fell madly in love, all those years ago.

As Ruth Allen explains it: 'Iain and I were a couple for five years, and married for just one of those. We stuffed it up, and divorced. But in terms of the restaurant, we never missed a beat. I think the mess we made of our marriage made us even more determined to make Tolarno work. We didn't want to lose that, as well.'

Or as Iain tells it: 'One day, we simply closed the restaurant, did the food for the reception, got married, and had the party at Ruth's parents' place.

'And years later, long after we had divorced, I remember Ruth's father coming up to me and saying: "Never mind. It was a great party."'

Which it was. And continues to be. And if you want to know why, look no further than those magical, mystical paintings on the walls of Tolarno Bistro. And at the magical, mystical, mischievous woman who put them there.

Daube de Boeuf à la Provençale
Steak Tartare with Parmesan
& Garlic Toasts
Tournedos au Poivre Vert
Entrecôte Minute et Beurre Café de Paris
Filet de Boeuf à la Ficelle
Chateaubriand Sauce Béarnaise
Le Bar Burger
Filet de Porc Vallée d'Auge
French Bacon & Beans
Toulouse Sausages with Lentil &
Cabbage Stew
Choucroute Garnie
Côte de Porc Charcutière

BEEF
& Pork

'Bistro food is like a trusted friend. It is reliable, it is comfortable, it is easy. But Bistro is more than just cuisine. It's a way of life. It's about taking the time to savour a meal and enjoy the company of family and friends.'

Laura Washburn
Bistro, 2003

Daube de Boeuf à la Provençale
(Provençal Beef Stew)

1.5 kilo lean stewing steak	A day ahead, cut into large cubes, trimming any excess fat.
1 celery stalk, diced 1 onion, finely chopped 1 medium carrot, diced 3 garlic cloves, crushed 1 crumbled bay leaf zest of 1 orange 3 tbsp olive oil 1 ½ cups dry white wine 6 tbsp brandy	Combine with beef, mix well and refrigerate overnight, stirring every now and then.
4 tbsp plain flour olive oil	The next day, preheat oven to 160°C. Drain beef, reserving liquid and vegetables. Flour beef, heat oil in a large heavy-bottomed pot or casserole, and brown meat in 2 or 3 lots.
1 x 2 cm thick piece of rindless bacon, cut into lardons (page 193) 12 button mushrooms, wiped with a damp cloth & quartered	Wipe out pot and heat fresh oil. Then toss in bacon and mushrooms and cook for a few minutes. Return beef and reserved marinade to pot.
2 x 400 gm cans diced tomatoes, drained a little 1–2 cups beef stock, bought (low salt) or homemade (page 254)	Add tomatoes, and just enough stock to cover. Bring to simmer, cover and put in bottom third of oven. Cook for 2–2 ½ hours or until meat is very tender, adding more stock if needed.
12 anchovies, mashed 3 tbsp balsamic vinegar 3 tbsp olive oil 3 garlic cloves, crushed 4 tbsp chopped fresh parsley	Mash together to form a paste and mix into the casserole for the last 30 minutes of cooking.
Creamy Mash (page 209)	Serve on mash.

Serves 6–8

Steak Tartare with Parmesan & Garlic Toasts

600 gm fillet steak, trimmed of all fat & sinew sea salt & freshly ground pepper	With a sharp knife, chop very finely. Put in a bowl and season fairly generously.
2 egg yolks 2 tbsp Dijon mustard 4 anchovies, finely chopped 1 tsp Worcestershire sauce 2 tsp tomato ketchup 2 tsp brandy a good splash or two of Tabasco 50 gm drained & finely chopped capers 50 gm cornichons (baby gherkins), finely chopped 2 tbsp chopped fresh parsley 1 small onion, finely chopped ¼ cup vegetable oil	Put ingredients in another bowl and mix well. Then combine with beef, mixing well. Centre a large pastry cutter on a well-chilled main course plate, spoon in beef mixture, smooth top and remove cutter. Repeat for remaining 5 plates. (Instead of mixing egg yolks in, you can, in a more traditional manner, make a small indent in the top of each patty and top with a yolk.)
150 gm unsalted butter 6 garlic cloves, crushed	Combine in a small pot, melt butter with garlic and set aside for 10 minutes.
8 slices toast bread, crusts removed & halved freshly grated parmesan	Brush bread generously with garlicky butter and panfry until golden. Toss in a bowl with parmesan while still hot. Serve alongside Steak Tartare.

Serves 6

'For some reason I didn't ever serve Steak Tartare. Maybe I was scared off by the rather peasanty boyfriend of one of my waiters who had put on a bit of a tantrum when told in a restaurant that he couldn't have it well done. Still, a very popular menu choice during the Massoni period where they served it with fries. This version comes from Anthony Bourdain's "Les Halles Cookbook" and, of course, it could be served with just plain toast, or even fries, but I like these garlicky parmesan toasts even better.'

Tournedos au Poivre Vert
(Fillet Steak with Green Peppercorn Sauce)

olive oil a knob of butter	Heat in a heavy bottomed pan.
8 x 100 gm fillet steaks sea salt & freshly ground pepper	Season well with pepper and seal on both sides. Remove and salt.
1 medium onion, finely chopped 1 garlic clove, crushed	Add to pan and sauté until tender.
2 tbsp brandy	Add and light.
1 cup beef stock, bought (low salt) or homemade (page 254) ½ cup thickened cream 2 tbsp green peppercorns, drained & rinsed 1 heaped tbsp Dijon mustard 1 heaped tbsp chopped fresh parsley	When flame goes out, add to pan and simmer for 6–7 minutes. Then return steaks and cook gently to desired degree, turning a few times (and adding more stock if necessary).
Pommes Sautées (page 212)	Remove steaks to 4 plates and, if need be, reduce the sauce. Serve with sautéed potatoes and a green salad. Serves 4–6

'I am sure every bistro in the world has, at one time or other, featured a pepper steak – it's still delicious.'

Entrecôte Minute et Beurre Café de Paris
(Minute Steak with Café de Paris Butter)

½ tsp chopped fresh parsley
a pinch of paprika
a pinch of dried tarragon
½ tsp Dijon mustard
1 ½ tbsp tomato puree
2 garlic cloves, crushed
2 anchovies
½ tsp Keen's traditional curry powder
1 tsp capers, drained
1 tsp pitted black olives
250 gm soft unsalted butter

Whiz up everything but the butter in a food processor until smooth. Then add butter and mix until well incorporated.

---

fresh lemon juice
Tabasco
freshly ground pepper

Flavour to taste with lemon, Tabasco and pepper. Refrigerate. (The leftover butter can be rolled in foil and put in the freezer until next time.)

---

4 x 150 gm porterhouse or rump steaks, trimmed of all fat & sinew
sea salt & freshly ground pepper

Batten out steaks carefully to an even thickness. Season to taste.

---

olive oil spray

Preheat ridged grill or BBQ.
Spray steaks and cook over high heat to desired degree. Place on a plate.

Demi-glaze, heated (page 255)
chips, bought or homemade (page 211)

Top with demi-glaze, a large scoop of Café de Paris butter and serve chips alongside.

Serves 4

'The idea for this dish came from a restaurant in Geneva which was called "Café de Paris". It only served a salad to start, with a terrific tangy vinaigrette followed by a minute steak with Café de Paris butter and a big pile of fries. There was no other choice but the place was packed.'

Filet de Boeuf à la Ficelle
(Poached Fillet of Beef on a String)

750 gm centre cut piece of beef fillet, trimmed of all fat & sinew	Cut into 4 even pieces. Tie each with kitchen string leaving a 15 cm tail end.
2 + litres beef stock, bought (low salt) or homemade (page 254)	Put in a high-sided pot, enough to fill three-quarters of the way up, and bring to the boil.
4 baby carrots 4 baby turnips 4 baby potatoes 4 baby beetroot	Peel. Put in pot and simmer, removing when tender. Then tie strings from beef onto 2 wooden spoons ensuring that beef will be suspended in centre of liquid. Place spoons, one across the other, on top of the pot. Cook meat gently for 7–8 minutes for medium rare (or to desired degree). Remove and keep warm.
chopped fresh parsley sea salt Dijon mustard cornichons (baby gherkins)	Take out a few cups of stock and reduce by one-third over high heat. Return vegetables to reheat. Slice beef and put into flat soup bowls along with vegetables and reduced stock. Sprinkle with parsley and serve with sea salt, mustard and cornichons on the side.

Serves 4

'I remember the first time I ordered this in a French bistro in Paris. The waiter repeated the order in English and I spent the next half-hour wondering what beef on a string could be. (I must admit my imagination was working overtime and, by the time this delicious poached beef arrived, I was convinced that I was getting some unmentionable part of the beast, too horrible to be called by its real name.)'

Châteaubriand Sauce Béarnaise
(Roasted Fillet of Beef with Béarnaise Sauce)

300 gm unsalted butter	Preheat oven to 250°C. Melt in a small pot over low heat. Skim off any foam from top and pour into a jug leaving milky residues behind.
2 tbsp dried tarragon ½ cup dry white wine ½ cup tarragon vinegar ¼ red onion, finely chopped	Put in a pot and reduce by half. Cool slightly then put in a stainless steel bowl.
4 egg yolks sea salt & freshly ground pepper	Add yolks and put over a pot of simmering water. Whisk until slightly thickened. Remove from heat, whisk in butter little by little. Season béarnaise sauce to taste.
1 x 600–700 gm centre-cut piece of beef fillet, trimmed of all fat & sinew sea salt & freshly ground pepper Dijon mustard	Put beef in baking dish. Season and smear with a generous layer of mustard. Cook in oven to desired degree then rest in a warm spot for 5–10 minutes.
Gratin Dauphinois (page 212)	Slice beef into thick pieces and serve with any juices and the béarnaise. Serve with Gratin Dauphinois and vegetables of choice.

Serves 4

'I was thrilled when the Massonis put this on one of their early menus. There is something about roasted fillet of beef that has always appealed. And no wonder I have always had a weight problem because béarnaise is about my favourite sauce and I reckon I've eaten a river of it over the years.'

Kenny (or Scoop, as he was known around St Kilda) was an unconventional Tolarno regular. He had been homeless for years, and made the step outside the old bistro entrance his own.

Armed with a fag and a glass of red by Ruth Allen, Barney or Andy, Kenny would discuss, with anyone prepared to listen, everything from the state of the nation to the changes threatening St Kilda. He had been a photo-journalist who, according to his sister, had returned from Vietnam a changed man, and had taken to the streets. But he had style, and an acute sense of humour.

Wearing an orange hard-hat, he would imperiously stop trams, write importantly on a clipboard and, eventually, wave them on. It was a miracle he was never run over.

Kenny also mastered the closing-time heart attack – calling for an ambulance and, when it arrived, insisting he was much better. He would them ask to be dropped home – to his lean-to behind the George Hotel or, in later years, to the admirable Sacred Heart Mission.

Kenny was, in truth, a bit of a liability: his personal hygiene was approximate, and standing downwind was inadvisable. A carer from the Sacred Heart told how it would take three of them to get him into a shower. He would also collapse, after a drinking bout, across the Tolarno entrance, forcing patrons to step over him.

But we loved Kenny. And when Ruth Krawat and I were married in Catani Gardens in St Kilda, he materialised from the bushes where, apparently, he had spent the night, to present us with a salad bowl and servers as a wedding present.

Ruth Allen tells of her embarrassment when Kenny presented her with a handsome bouquet of flowers. Noting her discomfort, he confessed he had found them taped to a lamp post which, to Kenny, seemed a terrible waste.

Over 250 St Kilda friends attended Kenny's funeral. One member of the congregation came forward, kissed the coffin twice and delivered a moving eulogy for his mate, 'Ken'. During which it became apparent he had not known the deceased at all. Kenny would have approved.

Le Bar Burger
(The Tolarno Burger)

vegetable oil
1 onion, finely chopped
2 garlic cloves, crushed
750 gm minced beef
150 gm tomato chutney, bought or homemade (page 258)
2 eggs, lightly beaten
2 tbsp Worcestershire sauce
sea salt & freshly ground pepper

Preheat oven to 200°C.
Heat a little oil in a pan and sauté onion and garlic until tender. Then place in a bowl, add rest of ingredients and mix well. Form into 8 patties. Heat oil in a fresh pan and seal well on both sides. Put on a baking tray.

---

2 onions, finely sliced
a good pinch of sugar
grated tasty cheese

Heat a little oil in a large heavy-bottomed pot, add onions and sugar and sauté until caramalised. Put on patties, top with cheese and cook in oven for about 10 minutes until golden brown and cooked through.

---

8 burger buns, cut in half
Dijon Mustard Aïoli (page 256)
Beetroot Chutney (page 257)
Tomato Chutney (page 258)
8 baby cos lettuce leaves
8 thick slices fresh tomato
8 slices rindless bacon

When burgers are ready, toast buns and grill bacon. Smear bun bottoms with aïoli then top with beetroot chutney, lettuce, fresh tomato, burger patty, bacon and tomato chutney. Press lid on firmly.

---

chips, bought or homemade (page 211)

Serve with a pile of chips alongside.

Serves 8

'By far Tolarno's most popular main course, there was a group of customers called the "Burger Boys" who came in every Friday night and had – what else? – burgers. And then there was Deano who once managed to eat ten of the mini versions in one sitting – a record to the end.'

BEEF & PORK

Filet de Porc Vallée d'Auge
(Pork Fillet with Calvados & Glazed Apples)

3 tbsp butter 2 tbsp sugar 2–3 Granny Smith apples, peeled, cored & cut into wedges chicken stock, bought (low salt) or homemade (page 254	Melt butter in a large heavy-bottomed pan, add sugar and apples and toss well. Cook gently, adding stock, little by little, once apples are coloured. Cook until well glazed.
olive oil a good knob of butter 4 pork fillets, trimmed of all fat & sinew & halved crossways	Heat oil and butter in another large pan and seal pork on all sides over high heat. Remove and set aside.
1 onion, finely chopped 1 medium carrot, diced 2 celery stalks, diced ¼ cup Calvados (French apple brandy) ½ cup dry white wine 1 cup chicken stock, bought (low salt) or homemade (page xx)	Add vegetables to pan and cook gently until tender. Add Calvados and ignite. When flames go out, add white wine and reduce quite heavily. Then add stock and bring to simmer. Place pork on top, cover and simmer until pork is cooked (keep a little pink in the centre). Remove pork and keep warm.
1 cup thickened cream 2 tbsp chopped fresh parsley sea salt & freshly ground pepper	Add to pan and reduce until sauce is formed. Slice pork and put on plates, spoon sauce over and serve glazed apples on the top.

Serves 4

'This dish is from Normandy, which is famous for its butter, apples and cream (and of course its Calvados).'

French Bacon & Beans

500 gm haricot beans	Soak overnight in cold water. Drain well.
1.5 kilo piece of bacon 2 bay leaves 2 garlic cloves, crushed 2 sprigs fresh thyme freshly ground pepper 3 litres chicken stock, bought (low salt) or homemade (page 254)	Put, along with beans, in a large heavy-bottomed pot. Bring to the boil, turn down to simmer and cook for 30 minutes, skimming regularly.
12 baby potatoes, peeled 12 baby (pickling) onions, peeled 3 medium carrots, peeled & cut into thick slices	Add and cook for another 30 minutes until beans and vegetables are tender. Remove bacon and thyme.
½ savoy cabbage, cleaned & cut into 6–8 wedges 1 cup frozen peas sea salt & freshly ground pepper	Add, stir and cook for about 10 minutes. Check seasoning.
chopped fresh parsley French grain mustard	Slice bacon and put into large flat soup or pasta bowls. Top with vegetables, stock and chopped parsley. Serve with mustard on the side.

Serves 6

'Halfway between a hearty soup and a braise, we served it, for a period, as a luncheon option.'

Toulouse Sausages with Lentil & Cabbage Stew

2–3 cups green lentils sea salt	Cook in plenty of salted water until tender. Drain and refresh under cold water then whiz up one-third in a processor.
2 tbsp butter 1 onion, chopped 1 garlic clove, crushed	Melt butter in a pot, add onion and garlic and cook until tender.
1 large zucchini, diced 1 medium carrot, diced 1 leek, white part only, washed well & diced ¼ savoy cabbage, finely shredded 2 cups beef stock, bought (low salt) or homemade (page 254) ¼ cup dry white wine	Add, along with whole lentils, and cook for 10 minutes. Then add pureed lentils and cook for another 10 minutes.
red wine vinegar Dijon mustard sea salt & freshly ground pepper 2 tbsp chopped fresh parsley	Flavour to taste with vinegar and mustard. Season to taste and mix in parsley.
8 Toulouse sausages (or similar)	Blanch in simmering water until firmish to the touch, then barbecue or grill until well coloured.
Dijon mustard	Serve sausages on a bed of lentils with mustard on the side. Serves 4

To Take Home
Iain's Sauces & Spice mixes $4

Iain Hewitson's
BAR & BISTRO AT
TOLARNO

PARTIES of most shapes and sizes — 3 rooms to choose from

SNACKS

* JACKET FRIES.. fried baby potatoes with a lightly spiced tomato relish & sour cream $7.50
* PARMESAN CRUMBED POLENTA CHIPS $5.   * BLOODY MARY OYSTER SHOOTERS $3.
* CRUMBED MUSHROOMS, Sce. Tartare $7.50   * NACHOS, with the works $7.50
* FRESHLY BAKED HOUSE BREAD, with a sundried tomato butter $1. per piece
* A TRIO of MEDITERRANEAN DIPS, with our flat bread $7   * House pickled onions. 4oz

ENTREES

* LASAGNE of roasted pumpkin, spinach & ricotta w. sage brown butter & italian parmesan $11.50
* CRISPY FRIED SARDINE FILLETS, with housemade sweet chilli sauce $11.
* A DOUBLE BAKED HEIDI GRUYERE SOUFFLE, with a blue mascarpone cream $11.
* A SALAD of COS LETTUCE, with grilled bacon, poached egg, parmesan, cheese straws and a Caesar dressing $11.
* PEPPERED POTATO GNOCCHI, with a lamb, spinach & mushroom ragu $10.50
* SOUTHERN INDIAN STEAMED FISH, cooked in banana leaves w. green coconut chutney coating - served with mint raita $12.50
* CARPACCIO of TASMANIAN SALMON, with olive oil, soy, chilli & garlic $13.50
* SOUP of THE DAY $7.
* GRILLED TASMANIAN OYSTERS, with a garlic butter & cheese crust $9 (6) $17.50 (12)
* HUEY'S KICK ARSE CHICKEN TORTILLA, with avocado salsa $11.50

MAINS

* RARE FILLET of MARINATED KANGAROO, with turkish eggplant salad $19
* TIM'S CHICKEN & VEGIE POT PIE, with polenta & corn crust & buttered green beans $17.50
* MOROCCAN HERB MARINATED CHICKEN BREAST, with olive oil roasted root vegetables and harissa yoghurt $17.50
* CHARGRILLED FRESH FILLET of FISH, on a bed of sautéed cabbage, bacon and onion with sauce béarnaise $18.
* A CHEESE & ROASTED VEGETABLE PASTIE, with bar room slaw & our apple chutney $14.
* CHARGRILLED OX TONGUE, with vegies in a port wine & wine vinegar sauce $11.50
* BRAISED LAMB SHANKS, on sweet potato mash w. a red capsicum & olive sauce $17.50
* AN OLD FASHIONED SHEPHERD'S PIE, cheese crusted & served with cabbage $12.50
* OUR FAMOUS BAR BURGER $7.50   * AN ITALIAN VEGETABLE BURGER $7.50 (with fries add another buck fifty)
* LAMB SNAGS, with creamy mash and our baked bean sauce $13.
* HOKKIEN NOODLES, either vegetarian $13 or with chicken & chinese sausage $16. in soy, garlic & chilli sauce with condiments on the side
* STEAK, MASH & ONIONS, chargrilled porterhouse with slow roasted balsamic onions, creamy mash and maitre d'hotel butter (cooked no more than medium) $20.
* PEPPERED PORTERHOUSE SALAD, on a bed of tomato & leaves with dijon mustard aioli (cooked no more than medium) $17.50

EXTRAS

* a garden salad $4   * a salad of green leaves $3.50   * greek salad $4.50
* fries $3.50   * polenta chips $5.   * a bowl of buttered vegetables $5.

Choucroûte Garnie
(Sauerkraut in the Style of Alsace)

1.5 kilos sauerkraut	Wash in cold water and drain in colander.
½ cup duck fat or lard 2 onions, chopped	Heat fat in large heavy bottomed pot and sauté onion until tender.
10 juniper berries, lightly crushed 1 garlic clove, crushed 6 whole black peppercorns 1 sprig of fresh thyme 1 bay leaf 6 whole coriander seeds 750 ml sparkling white wine	Add, along with sauerkraut, and mix well.
600 gm bacon, in the piece 4 slices smoked pork loin, on the bone preferably 2–3 cups chicken stock, bought (low salt) or homemade (page 254)	Add meat along with stock and cook very gently, covered, for about $1\frac{1}{2}$ hours, adding more stock if drying out. Remove meat and cut into largish pieces.
4 boudin blanc (French white sausages) 4 thick frankfurters 8–16 baby potatoes, peeled & parboiled	When almost ready, in another pot, gently simmer in water until hot. Then drain and cut sausages into large pieces.
French grain mustard	Place sauerkraut on a platter, place meats and potatoes around and serve with mustard on the side.

Serves 8

Côte de Porc Charcutière
(The Pork Butcher's Chops)

sea salt & freshly ground pepper 4 pork loin chops, about 2.5 cm thick	Rub salt and pepper into pork.
juice of 1 lemon 3 tbsp olive oil 1 garlic clove, crushed 2 tbsp chopped fresh parsley	Mix together, pour over pork and toss well. Put in the fridge for 3–4 hours. Then dry the chops with kitchen paper towels.
4 tbsp olive oil a dollop of butter	Preheat oven to 190°C. Heat oil and butter in a frying pan or casserole dish which can go into the oven. Then brown chops on both sides, in 2 lots. Set aside.
1 small onion, finely chopped 2 garlic cloves, crushed 6 button mushrooms, wiped clean & sliced	Throw into pan and sauté until tender, scraping up any brown bits with a wooden spoon.
1 tbsp plain flour	Add, turn down heat, and cook for a few minutes, stirring well.
½ cup dry white wine	Add and reduce by half.
1 cup beef stock, bought (low salt) or homemade (page 254) 1 x 400 gm can diced tomatoes, drained a little sea salt & freshly ground pepper 1 heaped tbsp Dijon mustard	Add, mix well and boil for 5 minutes. Then put chops on top, cover, and put in lower third of oven. Cook for 12–15 minutes, turning every now and then (chops should still be lightly pink along the bone). Remove pork and keep warm.
6 cornichons (baby gherkins), sliced 2 tbsp chopped fresh parsley 2 tbsp drained & chopped capers	Add and simmer gently on top of stove for about 5 minutes. Place chops on plates and top with sauce.

Serves 4

Beaujolais Nouveau began life as the tipple of choice of Lyonnaise petanque players – exponents of a game that takes its appeal, in part, from the fact that it can be played one-handed, with the free hand available for holding a drink, a Gauloise, or even a member of the opposite sex. The light, fruity wine is released only weeks after harvest, and has long been regarded by petanquers as the perfect restorative after their not especially physical exertions.

The drink's popularity spread from Lyon to Paris where it became a huge hit in bistros. (Beaujolais, the mature version, had always been popular in Paris: it was reckoned, in fact, that more 'Beaujolais' was consumed in Paris each year than was produced in ten years in Beaujolais itself.)

The popularity of the Nouveau was reinforced by a French government decree that it could be released only in the Beaujolais region, and not before the stroke of midnight on 15 November each year. According to local vignerons, this was when it was at its best. It was also widely believed that should there be any left by Easter, it should be poured down the drain. Which it seldom is.

The improbable global success of Beaujolais Nouveau can be put down to a Fleet Street journalist who, after noticing its popularity in France upon returning to London, decided to offer a small prize for the first member of the English wine trade who entered his office brandishing a bottle of the new vintage.

And so the Great Beaujolais Race was born, and mayhem ensued: English celebrants raced the stuff back from Beaujolais in everything from vintage racing cars, balloons and rowing boats to Ferraris and Rolls-Royces. And it was mandatory, naturally, to dispatch a few bottles of the dangerously drinkable stuff before and during the return journey.

Before long, the frivolous concept reached Australia. My former business partner, Sig Jorgensen, and I started the Clichy Cup when we owned the Melbourne restaurant of that name, and a number of vinous diehards, including my brother Don who brought a case to Melbourne in his baggage, began a new tradition.

Eventually, however, the French government tired of mad dogs and Englishmen hurtling down their motorways, sozzled. So they decided to release the wine worldwide on the same day, knocking the race concept neatly on the head.

At Tolarno, however, we kept the tradition alive with our midnight Nouveau parties, during which our regulars (and a few people we had never seen before) attempted to drink Australia's entire stock of Beaujolais Nouveau before dawn. And when they began to get very close to achieving this, we decided enough was enough, and called a halt.

Also, as a former Grand Conseil de l'Ordre du Beaujolais, which I was, I sniffily decided that by the time the young wine was shipped rather than air-freighted or driven by Bugatti to Australia, it had lost its freshness and much of its appeal.

Salade Lyonnaise
Peppered Porterhouse Salad
Salade Niçoise
Salade de Saucisson Pistache et Pommes de Terre
Salade Frisée aux Lardons et Oeufs Pochés
Salade de Tomates
Salade Aixoise
Tolarno's Caesar Salad
Salade Nouvelle
Épinards à la Crème
Petits Pois à la Française
Slow Roasted Onions with Olive Oil & Wine Vinegar
Roasted Sweet Potato Mash
Choux de Bruxelles à la Crème
Tian Provençale
Tomates à la Provençale
Purée de Panais
Creamy Mash
Pommes Boulangère
The Perfect Chips
Pommes Sautées
Gratin Dauphinois
Pommes Sautées à la Lyonnaise

SALAD
& Vegetables

'Take a little time in selecting your ingredients; go out of your way to find a really good butcher or cheesemaker or baker. Visit markets and rediscover the joy of eating locally grown produce in season, instead of food flown in from the other side of the world.'

Joanne Harris & Fran Warde
The French Kitchen, 2002

Salade Lyonnaise
(A Salad in the Style of Lyon)

2–4 thick pork sausages (pork & pistachio would be great)	Cook in just simmering water until firmish when squeezed. Remove.
8 waxy baby potatoes (kipflers, pink eyes or similar), peeled & halved 16 green beans, topped, tailed & halved crossways	Add potatoes to sausage water and cook until just tender, adding beans towards end. Drain well.
olive oil 1 x 2 cm thick piece of rindless bacon, cut into lardons (page 193)	Heat oil in a large heavy-bottomed pan. Slice sausage thickly and add, along with bacon. Sauté until crispy around edges.
½ punnet cherry tomatoes, halved 2 good handfuls of baby cos leaves Mustard Vinaigrette (page 256)	Put tomatoes and cos in a large bowl along with potatoes and beans. Add sausage and bacon, along with any pan juices. Toss with vinaigrette to taste.
baguette	Serve along with plenty of crusty bread.

Serves 4

Peppered Porterhouse Salad

olive oil
cracked black pepper
4 x 180 gm porterhouse steaks, trimmed of all fat & sinew
sea salt

Rub a ridged grill or BBQ with oil and preheat.
Put cracked pepper on a plate and press steaks firmly into it on both sides. Cook to the desired degree on grill. Season with salt and rest for 5 minutes before slicing.

2 good handfuls mixed lettuce leaves
4 large ripe red tomatoes, cored & thickly sliced
balsamic vinegar
Dijon Mustard Aïoli (page 256)

Arrange lettuce leaves neatly on 4 plates. Place tomato in a circle in centre of leaves. Sprinkle with balsamic and olive oil. Top with sliced steaks and any juices and sprinkle with aïoli.

Serves 4

'If you happen to have demi-glaze (page 255) or similar, a ladleful over the beef before topping with the aïoli makes this dish even more special.'

Salade Niçoise

(A Salad in the Style of Nice with Fresh Tuna)

4 x 180 gm tuna steaks, trimmed of all bloodline olive oil a squeeze of fresh lemon juice sea salt & freshly ground pepper	Preheat ridged grill or BBQ. Put tuna on a plate. Add a generous slurp of oil, lemon juice and seasoning. Toss a few times and set aside.
¾ cup Homemade Mayonnaise (page 256) 4 anchovies a splash of hot water	Whiz up in a food processor and set aside.
8 baby potatoes, peeled & halved 16–20 small green beans, topped & tailed	Boil potatoes in lightly salted water until tender, adding beans for the last few minutes. Drain well and put in a bowl.
4 hard-boiled eggs, peeled & quartered 1 punnet cherry tomatoes, halved 16 black olives, pitted a handful of baby cos leaves Mustard Vinaigrette (page 256)	Add to bowl with vinaigrette to taste, then mound on 4 plates.
chopped fresh parsley	Grill tuna steaks to no more than medium. Put on top of salad and flick mayonnaise over the lot (serve any extra on the side). Serves 4

'Oh all right, I know this is not terribly authentic, but it is delicious nonetheless.'

Salade de Saucisson Pistache et Pommes de Terre
(Pistachio Sausage & Potato Salad)

2–4 French pork & pistachio sausages	Poach in simmering water until firmish when squeezed. Turn off heat and leave in water.
8 waxy baby potatoes (kipflers, pink eyes or similar), peeled	Boil in another pot of salted water until almost tender. Drain and, when cool enough to handle, carefully cut into fairly thick slices.
olive oil	Heat a thin layer of oil in a large heavy-bottomed pan. Peel and slice sausage and cook until crusty. Remove and keep warm. If need be, add more oil and cook potatoes on both sides until golden.
a good handful of frisée lettuce, washed well & dried snipped fresh chives Mustard Vinaigrette (page 256) baguette	Toss potato, sausage, frisée and chives with a generous amount of vinaigrette. Put in 4 bowls or 1 large one and serve with plenty of sliced baguette to mop up the vinaigrette.

Serves 4

'Pork and pistachio sausages are available in French butchers or some gourmet delis (we buy ours from La Parisienne in the Melbourne suburb of Carlton). But you could use a good quality plain pork sausage instead.'

Salade Frisée aux Lardons et Oeufs Pochés
(Curly Endive Salad with Bacon & Poached Egg)

3 good handfuls of frisée lettuce, washed, dried & torn into pieces	Put in a large bowl.
olive oil 1 x 2 cm thick piece of rindless bacon, cut into lardons (see below)	Heat a little oil in a pan and fry until crispy around the edges. Remove from heat.
¼ cup Mustard Vinaigrette (page 256)	Add to pan off heat, toss well and pour over frisée. Toss salad well and mound on 4 plates or bowls.
white vinegar 4 large eggs Mustard Vinaigrette, extra	Bring a deep-sided pan of water to the boil. Turn down to gentle simmer. Add a splash of vinegar. Break eggs into cups then swirl water in a circle with a spoon before floating eggs into it. Cook until set then drain well. Put an egg on top of each salad and sprinkle with a little more vinaigrette. Serves 4

'One of the most famous bistro salads, I have eaten this on many occasions both in France and at Tolarno. To cut the bacon into lardons you simply cut across about 1 cm thick and then in half again lengthways.'

Salade de Tomates
(Tomato Salad)

4-6 ripe, red tomatoes, cored & sliced	Place on a large plate to cover.
4 heaped tbsp Homemade Mayonnaise (page 256) 2 tbsp buttermilk a splash of Tabasco a splash of Worcestershire sauce 2 tbsp freshly grated parmesan 2 anchovies, chopped	Place in a bowl and whisk well, adding a little hot water if too thick.
extra virgin olive oil sea salt & freshly ground pepper torn basil leaves	Sprinkle tomatoes with a little oil and seasoning, then flick dressing over generously and scatter with the basil. Serves 4

'If the tomatoes aren't fantastic, forget it.'

Ruth and I had hired a new waiter. His references had been checked, he seemed personable enough and, according to him, his waiting skills were second to none.

And indeed, all went swimmingly until one of the regulars ordered a very special bottle of wine. Now, these wines were always served in grand, Riedel glasses – large enough, almost, to hold a bottle in each glass. And this, improbably, was what our hero decided to demonstrate.

He showed the bottle with a flourish, opened it, poured a taste and then proceeded to divide the entire bottle between two glasses at the table for four. Whereupon he asked the host whether or not he would like another bottle.

Now, I was in two minds about this performance: should I fire him on the spot for gross incompetence, or reward him for this highly original approach to selling more wine?

Commonsense prevailed, of course, and he was banished from Tolarno for ever more.

Mind you, finding staff who matched the spirit of Tolarno had never been easy, as Georges Mora had discovered in the early 1970s after having placed an advertisement in a daily newspaper for a 'waitress, experienced and charming', and receiving not a single response.

'I think it was because it was the first time I had stipulated that she had to be charming,' Georges told a columnist on Melbourne's Sun-Pictorial the following week. And he was probably right.

Salade Aixoise
(A Specialty from Aix-en-Provence)

6–8 baby potatoes, scrubbed well & halved or quartered
16–20 baby green beans, topped & tailed
12-16 thin asparagus spears, tips only
1 cup double peeled broad beans (page 55)
sea salt

Boil potatoes in lightly salted water until tender, adding beans and asparagus for the last minute and broad beans for the last few seconds. Drain well and put in a large bowl.

---

3 hard boiled eggs, peeled & quartered
1 yellow capsicum, cored, seeded & finely sliced
4 olive-oil preserved artichoke hearts, halved or quartered
4 ripe red tomatoes, cored & quartered
6 anchovies, chopped
12 small black olives
extra virgin olive oil
red wine vinegar
sea salt & freshly ground pepper

Add to bowl and toss carefully with oil, vinegar and seasoning to taste.

Basil Pistou (page 257)

Sprinkle generously over the top.

Serves 4–6

Tolarno's Caesar Salad

3–4 slices day-old sourdough bread olive oil 2 garlic cloves, crushed 2 tbsp finely grated parmesan	Remove crusts from bread, and cut into 1.5 cm croutons. Heat a layer of oil along with garlic in a large pan and, over moderate heat, pan-fry croutons until golden all over. Drain well and toss in a bowl with parmesan.
6 slices prosciutto	Add to pan and cook until shrivelled. Drain well and, when crisp, break each slice into 3 or 4 pieces.
½ cup Homemade Mayonnaise (page 256) 3–4 anchovies, chopped 1 tsp Dijon mustard a squeeze of fresh lemon juice	Combine along with a little hot water, if necessary, to make into a dressing consistency.
3 heads baby cos lettuce or the tender inner leaves of 3 large cos lettuces freshly grated parmesan	Wash and dry leaves in a salad spinner. Toss in a bowl with croutons, prosciutto, parmesan and dressing to taste. Mound in 4 flat soup bowls.
4 poached eggs (page 66) chopped fresh parsley	Nestle an egg in each salad and sprinkle with parsley.

Serves 4

'How could you have a bistro cookbook without a Caesar recipe?'

Salade Nouvelle
(Liver, Spinach & Bacon Salad with Mustard Vinaigrette)

olive oil 16–20 duck or chicken livers, cleaned sea salt & freshly ground pepper	Heat oil to smoking in a large pan then, without overcrowding, put livers in one layer (this can be done in 2 or 3 lots if necessary). Cook until crusty on the outside and pink within. Remove and put in a bowl.
2–3 rashers rindless bacon, chopped	Throw bacon in pan and sauté until crispy around the edges. Remove from heat.
½ cup Mustard Vinaigrette (page 256) 2 good handfuls of baby spinach leaves, washed & dried	Add vinaigrette to pan, swirl around and add to bowl along with spinach. Toss well and serve either in one large or 4 individual bowls. Serves 4

'I first had this dish in the quintessential French bistro, Leon de Lyon, in (where else?) Lyon. It has been a favourite ever since.'

Épinards à la Crème
(Creamed Spinach)

1.5 kilos fresh spinach leaves washed, stems removed	Put in a large colander in 3 or 4 lots. Pour boiling water over top and toss well to ensure all is wilted. Drain very well and, when cool enough to handle, squeeze dry with your hands and chop finely.
3 tbsp butter 2 tbsp plain flour	Heat butter in a large heavy-bottomed pot and add spinach. Toss well for a few minutes then add flour. Mix well and cook over low heat for a few minutes.
1 cup thickened cream sea salt freshly grated nutmeg	Add cream, salt to taste and a grating of nutmeg. Simmer for 5 minutes until slightly thickened.

Serves 6

'A very popular accompaniment when I first began working in French restaurants, I remember spending half the day cleaning and cooking the bloody stuff because, as we know, spinach, when cooked, shrinks away to nothing.'

During our years at Tolarno Bistro, Ruth Allen tired of being asked whether Huey was in tonight. So during table service she began calling out things like: 'Come on Huey, hurry up with that salad,' or even 'Huey, sweep that kitchen floor,' and so on, when I was somewhere else at the time. I could not, obviously, assess how effective this was. But given the modest size of the hatch between the kitchen and the bistro, I can only assume there were a few sore necks as patrons craned to see whether I was really on the salad section, or sweeping the floor. Which I wasn't. But then, perhaps this is just my ego talking: perhaps they didn't care whether I was there or not, and one or two of them may even have thought the food was better when I was away.

Also, long-term master of Le Bar, Barney Allen, Ruth's brother and a key ingredient of Tolarno, was sorely missed by his devoted regulars whenever he took a holiday. Other staff members, on those occasions, would quickly tire of the Barney question and would write a sign to the effect that Barney was on holidays, and that they would get very pissed off if anyone asked about him again, or even mentioned his name, thanks very much.

And speaking of Barney, a legendary moment in his life came when he decided to abandon Le Bar after pressure from his parents on completing his accounting degree. Devastated, but eternally grateful for his contribution, Ruth and I presented him with a bottle of Penfolds Grange, from a fine year, as a going-away present. But imagine my surprise when, the following day, I arrived at Tolarno to find Barney behind Le Bar. He was back, he informed me, and he remained behind the bar until our tenure ended.

I often ask Barney for the bottle of Grange back but, somehow, I don't think I am ever going to get it. I reckon the ungrateful bugger drank it.

Petits Pois à la Française
(Fresh Peas with Lettuce, Onion & Bacon)

1 crisp heart of iceberg lettuce	Wash carefully, dry and shred.
1 bunch spring (green) onions	Cut white and lower green part into 3 cm lengths.
1 x 2 cm thick piece of bacon, cut into thin lardons (page 193) 6 tbsp unsalted butter	Put in a pot and cook for a few minutes.
½ cup water 1 tbsp sugar sea salt & freshly ground pepper 2 tbsp chopped fresh parsley 3 cups shelled fresh peas (about 1.5 kilos unshelled)	Add along with lettuce and spring onion and toss well. Cover pot and cook gently for 20 minutes or so until very tender. Check seasoning. Serves 4–6

'Always on the menu during the days of Leon and Vivienne. I invariably ordered a portion just for myself and got very upset if anyone wanted to share.'

Slow-roasted Onions With Olive Oil & Wine Vinegar

6 brown onions
olive oil

Preheat oven to 120°C.
Cut onions in half crossways, skin and all. Brush cut sides with oil and put in one layer, cut-side up, in a roasting tray and cook in oven for about 1 hour until caramelised and tender.

extra virgin olive oil
red wine vinegar
sea salt & freshly ground pepper
chopped fresh parsley

When cool enough to handle, peel and toss in a bowl with oil, vinegar, seasonings and parsley to taste. Serve warm or cold.

Serves 4

'Maggie Beer prepared these on one of my shows many years ago. She served them barbecued kangaroo but they also work brilliantly with any grilled or barbecued meat.'

Roasted Sweet Potato Mash

4 large sweet potatoes, scrubbed

Preheat oven to 200°C.
Put sweet potatoes in a roasting tray and bake until tender (about 40 minutes). Take out and, when cool enough to handle, peel and whiz up in a food processor.

125 gm soft unsalted butter
sea salt & freshly ground pepper
1 tbsp chopped fresh parsley

Add and whip with a wooden spoon.

Serves 8

Choux de Bruxelles à la Crème
(Creamed Brussels Sprouts)

16–20 brussels sprouts, cleaned sea salt	Bring a large pot of salted water to the boil and blanch sprouts for 3–4 minutes. Drain well and, when cool enough to handle, slice thinly lengthways.
olive oil a knob of butter sea salt & freshly ground pepper	Heat oil and butter until foaming then throw in the sprouts, season and cook, tossing regularly, for a few minutes.
½ cup thickened cream 2 tbsp chopped fresh parsley	Add and cook until cream has almost disappeared and sprouts are very tender.

Serves 4

'I know people either love or hate brussels sprouts, but most people find this dish delicious – just don't tell the haters what they are eating.'

Tian Provençale
(Eggplant, Onion & Tomato Gratin)

olive oil 1 large onion, chopped 2 garlic cloves, crushed	Preheat oven to 190°C. Heat oil in a heavy-bottomed pot and sauté until tender.
3 x 400 gm cans diced tomatoes, drained a little 2 cups vegetable stock, bought (low salt) or homemade (page 254) sea salt & freshly ground pepper	Add and cook until reduced, thick and fragrant.
12 fresh basil leaves, torn 8 pitted black olives, sliced	Add and mix well. Set aside.
1 large eggplant, sliced olive oil spray	Preheat ridged grill. Spray eggplant and grill a few at a time until tender.
2 red onions, sliced 1 large red capsicum, cored, seeded & sliced	In a pan, heat a little oil and sauté until tender. Remove and set aside, leaving any oil behind.
2 cups fresh breadcrumbs made from day old sourdough bread 2 garlic cloves, crushed	Along with a little more oil, add to pan and cook until golden.
3 tbsp chopped fresh parsley	Mix into crumb mixture.
6 ripe, red tomatoes, sliced	Layer a gratin dish with eggplant sprinkled with a little more olive oil, then onion mix and half the tomato sauce. Top with sliced tomatoes, rest of tomato sauce and crumbs in an even layer. Spray with olive oil and cook in oven for 30 minutes until vegetables are tender and crumbs are golden brown. Serves 6–8

'A tian is a Provençal earthenware pot but any gratin dish will do.'

Tomates à la Provençale
(Gratinéed Tomatoes)

100 gm fresh breadcrumbs, made from 2-day-old sourdough bread
4 garlic cloves, crushed
4 tbsp chopped fresh parsley
juice & grated zest of 1 lemon

Preheat oven to 180°C.
Mix together.

---

8 ripe, red tomatoes, cored & halved
100 gm butter, melted

Place tomatoes cut-side up, in an oiled gratin dish. Carefully top each one with the crumb mix, pressing down firmly, and then spoon butter over. Cook in oven for about 30 minutes until tomatoes are tender and crumbs are browned.

Serves 4

'The same mix can also be placed on top of medium-sized field mushrooms but don't forget to peel them first.'

Purée de Panais
(Parsnip Mash)

1 kilo parsnips, peeled & cut into chunks sea salt milk	Put in a pot with salt and milk to cover. Cook until very tender. Drain well, reserving milk.
75 gm soft unsalted butter sea salt & freshly ground pepper	Mash, adding as much of the reserved milk as is necessary to make a smooth mixture. Whip in butter and season to taste.

Serves 6–8

Creamy Mash

1 kilo potatoes, peeled & quartered sea salt	Boil in salted water until tender then drain very well.
1 cup milk	Bring to the boil and, while mashing potatoes, add little by little.
½ cup thickened cream 75 gm soft unsalted butter sea salt & freshly ground pepper	Add and whip with a wooden spoon.

Serves 8

'If this sounds a little fattening, consider the current French fave – Paris Mash, which consists of equal quantities of potato and butter.'

Pommes Boulangère
(The Baker's Potatoes)

1 litre chicken stock, bought (low salt) or homemade (page 254)	Preheat oven to 190°C. Put in a pot and reduce over high heat by half
1 kilo baby potatoes, peeled & cut into 2 cm thick slices a good knob of butter 1 tsp fresh thyme leaves sea salt & freshly ground pepper	Add to stock and cook until potatoes are almost tender. Drain well, reserving stock.
olive oil 2 large onions, sliced 1 garlic clove, crushed 1 bay leaf	Heat a little oil in a heavy-bottomed pan and sauté until soft and golden.
1 tbsp chopped fresh parsley	Add to onion mixture. Then, in a gratin dish, layer potatoes and onions, finishing with potatoes. Pour reserved stock over the top.
butter	Dot with butter, cover loosely with foil and bake for 30 minutes. Then remove foil and cook for another 15–20 minutes or until golden on top.

Serves 4–6

'In the old days these potatoes would have been cooked, from raw, in the bottom of the baker's oven which was commonly used for communal cooking.'

The Perfect Chips

1 kilo potatoes, peeled	Cut into chips and immediately put in a bowl of iced water. Leave for at least 30 minutes, then put under running water until water runs clear. Then drain and pat dry.
6 cups vegetable oil or shortening	Heat in a deep-fryer or a deep pot with a frying thermometer to 130°C. Cook until soft but not coloured. Drain and cool.
kitchen towels sea salt	Reheat oil to 190°C. Without overcrowding, fry the chips until golden brown. Drain on kitchen towels and sprinkle over salt.

Serves 6

'My favourite potato varieties for chips are russet burbanks (which are also called Idahos) and kennebecs.

Pommes Sautées
(Classic Sautéed Potatoes)

1 kilo waxy baby potatoes (such as kipflers), peeled & cut into even chunks sea salt	Boil in lightly salted water for 5 minutes. Drain and cool a little. Then scrape surface all over with the prongs of a fork.
olive oil	Heat a thin layer in a large pan. Without overcrowding, in one layer, cook potatoes until crispy and tender. Drain well on kitchen paper towels, salt, and keep hot in oven while sautéeing the rest

Serves 6

Gratin Dauphinois
(A Creamy, Cheesy Potato Gratin)

600 ml thickened cream 1 bay leaf	Preheat oven to 170°C. Put in a large pot and reduce by one third.
1.5 kilos potatoes, finely sliced on a bench slicer sea salt & freshly ground pepper	Add and bring back to boil. Remove from heat.
soft unsalted butter sea salt & freshly ground pepper grated tasty cheese	Smear gratin dish with butter. Put half the potatoes in and season. Pour over some cream and then scatter over some cheese. Repeat process, finishing with cheese. Put in oven and cook for 45 minutes or until golden and very tender when pierced with a sharp knife.

Serves 6–8

Pommes Sautées à la Lyonnaise
(Sautéed Potatoes with Onions)

1 kilo waxy baby potatoes (such as kipflers), scrubbed	Cook in their skins until just tender. Drain and, when cool enough to handle, peel and cut into two or three pieces.
2 tbsp duck fat 2 onions, finely sliced a pinch of sugar sea salt & freshly ground pepper	Heat fat in a large pan, add onions, sugar and seasonings and cook until onions are golden.
2 tbsp duck fat	Remove onions and set aside. Add extra duck fat, heat then add potatoes and cook until well coloured. Return onions and cook, tossing, for another five minutes or so.
chopped fresh parsley	Sprinkle with parsley.

Serves 6

'Duck fat is fairly freely available at poulterers and good butchers. But if you can't find it, a mix of butter and olive oil works almost as well.'

A Day in the Life of TOLARNO

8 a.m. Nothing of consequence happens early in Fitzroy Street. And this is bloody early, whatever the rest of Melbourne might think. The street is not yet properly aired. The only real signs of life involve newsagents, commuters, tourists, fitness fanatics and other deviates. Including a wino who sits, crookedly, in a doorway – oblivious, apparently, to the chill that must be penetrating his open-toed Dunlop Volleys, and blinking painfully at the light as he tries to remember where he is. And why. And as he sits, he wonders how long it will take the late summer warmth, barely beginning to make its presence felt, to dry out his trousers.

Outside Tolarno, the tables and benches have not yet appeared. Which means that officially, as far as St Kilda is concerned, this day has not yet begun. There are, however, signs of life from a flat above Cacao, the chocolate shop just up the road, from which Ruth Allen emerges, just as the hour clicks into place. She collects a couple of croissants from downstairs. And then she heads for Tolarno where she slips worn keys into old locks and her day, her Tolarno day, gets under way.

The pastry chef arrives and flicks on the coffee machine. Today, it's Cam Cox, who has been with Huey and Ruth for about four years. Cam also does segment work for the

⊕ Cameron Cox

boss's cooking shows on the telly. And he's very good at it. But by trade, Cam is a pastry chef, and he arrives early to start work on the bread and pastries in general, and the all-important Tolarno burger buns – full-size and bite-size – in particular. Cam also takes care of desserts, something with which Huey has little patience and seldom eats, let alone cooks.

Coffee's up. Ruth, Cam and Robbie the cleaner gulp it down and discuss things. Robbie begins his three-hour clean, first by putting out the tables and benches to declare St Kilda open, then by setting about the bathrooms and Le Bar, which smells stale and a bit smoky, as a well-exercised bar should, and then by putting out the bottle bins. Ruth takes a peek into one of the bins, spots a few Estrella empties, and notes that Dean, a regular and the Tolarno mini-burger champ (he once managed ten, unassisted), was in last night. Ruth knows her regulars, their tipples and their foibles. Then she checks the bathrooms. In cases of extreme ugliness, she will always muck in, literally, to help Robbie get them sorted. And when there are syringes in the toilets, she pulls on gloves and retrieves them. The gents', she reckons, gets dirtier than the ladies'. But the ladies' gets messier. Could that be a metaphor for life in St Kilda? Probably not.

10 a.m. Ruth takes a long, hard look at the Tolarno bible – the bookings log. How are things shaping? How full will it be tonight? Are there bookings that need to be confirmed? Too many bookings for two? Twos, reckons Ruth, are not good for the bistro. They stuff up the atmosphere. The place needs a couple of big groups to power things along, and Ruth wrangles things like that. Even on Valentine's Day, when couples are the go everywhere else, she will allow only seven twos in the place. Hard woman, Ruth. Romance? Forgedaboudit.

11 a.m. Head chef Noel Kelly – that's a female Noel as in No-elle — is doing lunch, and arrives to fire up those parts of the kitchen Cam hasn't yet reached, and to

↪ Noel Kelly

advance the prep for lunch, for which the doors open at noon. Noel has been at Tolarno for eight years, so she knows the ropes – as does her admirable 2IC, Luke Grellis, the former Bendigo boy with whom she splits shifts. Noel, a Melburnian, started at Tolarno as an apprentice and advanced from there. The night before, Noel had to comfort an apprentice when details of the bistro's impending closure were revealed to staff. The apprentice, who had been involved just long enough to have fallen in love with the place, wept. Noel put an arm around her, and told her that her first restaurant had also closed at an inconvenient moment, and that life has a way of sorting these things out. Which is almost true.

12 p.m. The bistro is open for business and two male customers arrive. Andy Percy, bistro manager, is there to meet them. He can handle the floor on his own for lunch, and does so. The customers order with hardly a glance at the menu: one Thai chicken curry; one minute steak; a cos lettuce, bacon and parmesan salad to share. And a couple of glasses of red. Any red, thanks. Huey's selection will be fine. Yep, regulars.

Nobody else arrives for half an hour, and then it's a pair of out-of-towners. Two women of a certain age. A couple, perhaps. They stare at the menu long enough to suggest this is their first visit. Then they split an order of Tom Cooper's marvellous smoked salmon and follow that with bangers and mash and shepherd's pie. Good eaters, but not drinkers. Two waters. Sad, that. Nobody should have to drink water. Not in Tolarno, anyway. It's probably un-Australian or something.

A few more lunchers drift in, eat, and drift out again. A couple of bottles of mid-

◉ Andy Percy   ◉ Glenn Waugh

priced wine are ordered, opened and emptied, and a couple more shepherd's pies, a porterhouse steak and four burgers. Bloody burgers. The lunch trade does not set the world on fire, but the punters enjoy themselves. Especially the two women who may have been a couple. They say they love it here, and they would come all the time, except they live in Toowoomba. Huh?

2.30 p.m. The rest of the kitchen staff arrive and the five sections start to take shape – pastry, grill, stove, hot entrée, cold entrée. The kitchen is warming up, but not unpleasantly. Just busy warm. And the movement is anything but frantic at lunch. A doddle, really. But soon, prep is under way for the evening ahead.

4.30 p.m. Suddenly, there are five people in the kitchen, and they look busier. Also, Barney arrives, and the mood of the place improves. Barney Sunshine. (Barney Allen, actually – he's Ruth brother, and, according to Ruth, the nicest boy in the world. Few would argue with her assessment, and not just because she frightens the life out of them. Barney's a treasure. And a legend.) The gloriously named Denzil Shutie has also arrived. He is the washer-upper, the kitchen hand, and he aspires to no other job, although he can also handle the cold section, at a pinch. On Saturdays, there were two washer-uppers until Denzil joined the team. He insisted he could do it on his own, and he could, and he does, and he welcomes the extra money. He is, inexplicably, happy in his work. Ruth says he, too, is a treasure, except for the fact that when he is off sick, she has to hire two people to replace him. And also, nobody

⬆ Barney Allen

⬆ Denzil Shutie

WHEN CLEANING THE
SLICER, TURN DIAL
BACK TO ZERO,
OR ELSE YOU WILL
LOSE A FINGER!!
Thank-You

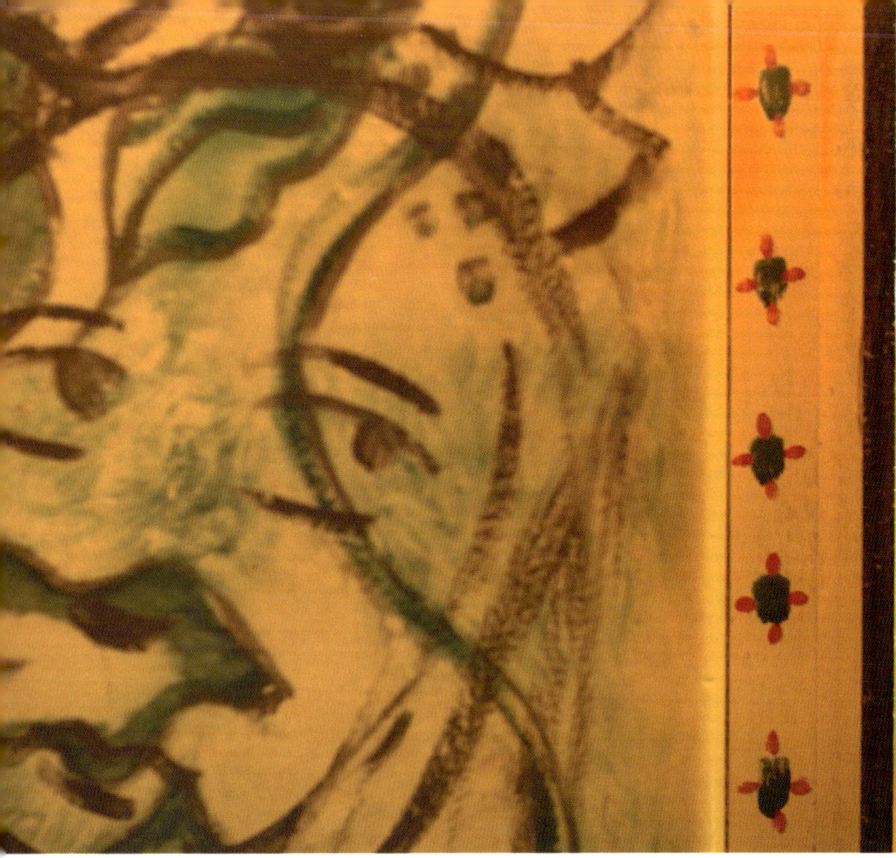

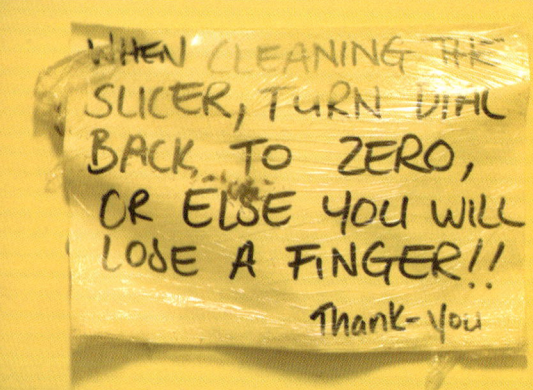

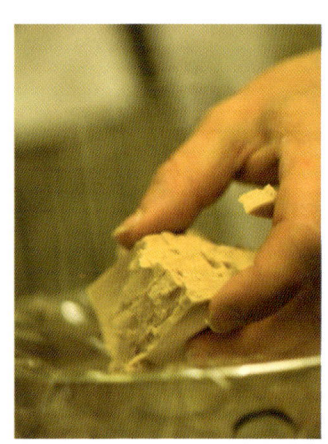

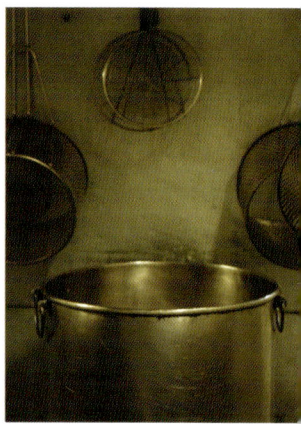

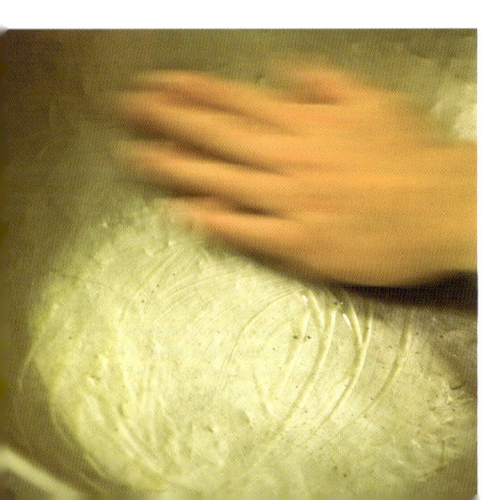

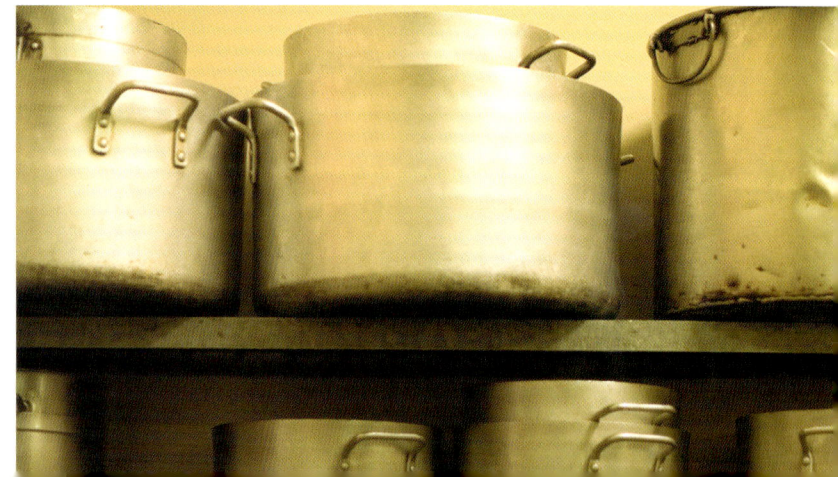

calls him Denzil Shutie. In Tolarno, he is Denzil Washingman. Cute.

6 p.m. Too late to turn back now. The first serious punters arrive and are shown to their table by one of the two floor staff, both of whom arrived at 4.30 pm to set up the bistro for service. They know the routine. There are no new chums in this place – everyone seems to have been working here forever, and they are proud of it. And even though they know it all has to end quite soon, probably in tears, nobody is thinking of leaving. They want to be here at the death. They can smell history, especially when there is a measure of decay involved. And they can detect a strong whiff of unenlightened greed in the air, and the stupidly and unnecessarily enforced death of an era.

8 p.m. The bistro is roaring. Not a spare seat, and the floor staff seem to have about four hands each. The food – robust and sensible – is flowing through the hatch that links the kitchen and the bistro, all of it carefully watched by Huey, who has assumed the orders position just inside the hatch. He can see in and he can see out. He misses nothing, and he keeps things rolling. Oysters, smoked salmon, bowl after bowl of French onion soup, mussels – still a tradition here after more than 40 years – and more.

10 p.m. There are replacements for some of the vacated seats – regulars, most of them, who would rather lose a finger than book at Tolarno. They wait in the bar, talking, drinking, until there is room. And when they find a place, the orders start to roll in all over again – lasagne, six more shepherd's

pies, porterhouse steak, more bloody burgers...

At a table of 8 pm arrivals, the savoury dishes have been cleared away and pavlovas have just landed in their places. And thought is being given to ordering a sauternes of a quality that may even cause the boss to rub his hands together. And in Le Bar, Barney is also doing fine work, as usual. Filling drink demands with his unique form of practised, casual precision, he is also taking food orders – burgers, crumbed mushies, polenta chips, tasting plates and still more burgers, especially the mini ones. And then he distributes these – some to customers in Le Bar who eat them there, others to occupants of the Barrel Room, a smoke-free environment for fussy breathers. Nobody need go hungry, and few ever do. Provided, of course, they order in time. Because the kitchen, ready or not, is about to close.

11 p.m. That's it. Food's over. And the serious business of cleaning the kitchen begins in earnest. This is venerable cooking equipment, battle-scarred, but it still has to gleam, more or less. And when the kitchen team have finished, they split into two groups – those who head home to sleep soundly, and those who adjourn to Le Bar to wind down, to keep Barney company, to take in the atmosphere or simply to get wasted and to wallow in the sounds which are starting to build as the iPod feeding the sound system does its finest work. There are outbreaks of spontaneous warbling, but this place is bursting with musicians – you'd better know your stuff if you are intending to get into that.

Midnight. The bar is heaving. There are around 60 people in there, all of whom seem to know each other. Or at least, they do now. There are running jokes, conversations that take place in shorthand, others that have clearly taken place before. Barney delivers the occasional cocktail to people who, sometime tomorrow, will wish they'd stuck to beer. The boss has been occupying his stool for just on an hour and he has that bleary-but-affable look about him that suggests this will be one of the better nights. Actually, it is already. Tom Waits is rasping from the iPod, and everyone here seems to like Tom Waits.

1 a.m. Closing time, which, coincidentally, is everyone's favourite Tom Waits album, but that's no excuse. The song playing is the Nick Cave version of 'Let It Be', and Huey leads the singing, insists Barney run the track again, and leads the singing one more time. Let it be, let it beeee... The bar is closed and glasses are retrieved. Those who want to be last to move try to get involved in a serious natter with the boss, but he is on to them and, in any case, is talking in Braille. Ruth is running down, off the top of her head, a list of the regulars who have been in tonight. Rob, of course, quietly and mysteriously, and all on his own. Grant, Tiny, Jen, Anthony, Grace, Rory, Greg, Josty, Beast, Jack the Lad, Milo, Horse, the Baron... and dozens more. Where will they all go when the dark day comes?

Rebecca is still there – a regular of fifteen years standing. She and several others, mainly musos, have that night undertaken the course that, in her opinion, must be completed regularly by every true St Kilderite. It has to start with a few drinks

in Le Bar, move on to Pint on Punt to catch the Large No. 12s, then on to the George public bar to sing along with the Billy Miller Beatles, then back to Le Bar with any hangers-on you have collected along the way. And when you arrive at Le Bar you have to eat at least one Tolarno burger, the big version, and sit through a monologue by the bar's resident clinical psychologist, Dr Bob, without screaming or tearing your hair.

You have to do these things because that's the way it is in St Kilda. And as far as the Tolarno regulars are concerned, that's the way it has always been. And now somebody is trying to tell them that St Kilda will have to manage without Tolarno. And without Le Bar and Barney and the burgers and Ruth and Dr Bob. Which makes no sense to them. Not that it has to make sense, of course. This is St Kilda. But also, this is bullshit, is it not, Dr Bob? St Kilda, shouts a bloke from the back of the bar, is fucked. Which may, of course, be part of its charm.

2 a.m. Le Bar is closed and the toilets are locked for the night. Down the way, near where a soup truck, hours earlier, has been taking care of necessities for those who through straitened circumstances have been denied the warmth and companionship of Tolarno, a wino folds himself into a neglected doorway, oblivious to the cold which must, surely, be beginning to find its way into his open-toed Dunlop Volleys...

Mousse au Chocolat
Pêche Melba
Crème Renversée au Caramel
Paris Brest
Crème Brûlée
*Oeufs à la Neige with Passionfruit
Anglaise & Orange Caramel*
Cam's Berry Pond
Tarte aux Pommes
Ed's Triple Chocolate Mousse Cake
*Mini Pavlovas with Passionfruit
Syrup & Fresh Fruit*
Cappuccino Soufflé
Clafoutis aux Pruneaux
*Crêpes Suzette with Banana &
Passionfruit Stuffing*
Tarte au Citron
A Trio of Ice-creams with Fresh Fruit
Poires à la Beaujolaise
Bande au Poires

DESSERTS

'The dawn of what we now know as French cuisine came in the unlikely form of a fourteen year old Italian girl, Catherine de Medici. Catherine, the great granddaughter of Lorenzo the Magnificent, came to France in 1533 to marry the Duke of Orleans, later to become King Henri II. So appalled by the food and eating habits of the French, she bought a battalion of Italian cooks as well as the herbs and vegetables with which they could produce the more delicate cuisine she had known in Italy.'

Barry Bone & Joanne Donsky
La Crème de la Crème, 1982

Mousse au Chocolat
(Chocolate Mousse)

250 gm top quality dark cooking chocolate (Valrhona or similar)	Break into pieces and melt in a heatproof bowl over simmering water.
½ cup thickened cream	Bring to the boil and whisk into chocolate until smooth. Cool for 5 minutes.
¾ cup thickened cream a splash of any fruit liqueur (such as framboise, cassis, Grand Marnier)	Whip until soft peaks form. Then fold in, little by little, into chocolate mixture. Put in 4 ramekins or soufflé dishes and refrigerate until firm.

Serves 4

'Chocolate mousse doesn't come much simpler than this – or more delicious. But because it is so simple it is dependent on the quality of the chocolate – only use the very best. And, remember, the bowl should never touch the simmering water otherwise the chocolate may seize.'

Pêche Melba
(Peach Melba)

50 gm caster sugar 1 litre water ½ cinnamon stick ¼ lemon, sliced	Put in a pot and stir until sugar dissolves.
4–8 fresh peaches, unpeeled	Add to syrup, weight with a plate and simmer very gently for 5 minutes. Turn off heat and leave to cool in syrup, turning frequently. When cool, peel, stone and halve. Return to liquid until needed.
2 punnets raspberries a splash of framboise (raspberry liqueur)	Whiz up in a blender with a little poaching liquid (adding a little extra sugar if necessary). Pass through a sieve.
Vanilla Bean Ice-cream, bought or homemade (page 259)	Place a couple of scoops of ice-cream in each glass. Top with peaches and a generous amount of raspberry sauce.

Serves 4

'If this sounds very simple, please consider the creator. Escoffier's recipe: "poach the peaches, dish them in a timbale upon a layer of vanilla ice-cream and coat them with raspberry puree".'

Crème Renversée au Caramel
(Cream Caramel)

75 gm caster sugar 100 ml warm water	Preheat oven to 165°C. To make caramel, cook sugar and water gently in a heavy-bottomed pot until golden, swirling now and again (don't stir).
2 cups milk 1 vanilla bean, halved lengthways & seeds scraped	At same time, place in another pot, gently bring to the boil and remove from heat.
4 large eggs 100 gm caster sugar	Whisk eggs in a bowl, add sugar all at once and whisk well until pale and thick.
	Place 4–6 dariole moulds in a baking dish and pour a little caramel into each. Then pour milk into egg mixture. Whisk well, strain and remove any foam. Pour into caramel-lined moulds. Pour boiling water in dish to come one-third of the way up sides of moulds. Cook in oven for 30–40 minutes until just set. Cool and refrigerate. Turn out to serve. Serves 4–6

'This version is from Tolarno pastry chef, Cameron Cox.'

Paris Brest
(Choux Pastry Cake Stuffed with Pastry Cream & Fresh Fruit)

2 cups water 2 tsp salt 240 gm unsalted butter	Preheat oven to 180°C. Bring to boil in a heavy-bottomed pot and cook until butter is melted.
2 cups plain flour	Remove pot from heat, add all at once and stir until paste is smooth. Don't overbeat; this should take only a few seconds. Cool for 5 minutes.
8 eggs	Transfer to the bowl of an electric mixer and add eggs, one at a time, mixing well between each addition. When all have been added, beat for a further 5 minutes, until smooth and glossy. Put in a piping bag and make a circular cake on a baking tray, by starting with a small circle in the centre and then continuously spiralling out in a circular pattern. Bake for 20–30 minutes until golden brown. Place on a rack and make a small hole in sides to allow steam to escape. Cool.
Crème Pâtissière (page 259) fresh fruit (berries, kiwi fruit, mango, fresh stone fruit, passionfruit, etc) icing sugar	Cut brest in 2 round layers. Smear bottom layer generously with pastry cream, top with fruit and replace top layer. Sprinkle with icing sugar. Serves 6–8

Crème Brûlée
(Glazed English Custard Cream)

2 vanilla beans, halved 300 ml thickened cream 200 ml milk	Preheat oven to 100°C. Scrape vanilla seeds into a heavy-bottomed pot, add cream and milk and bring to simmer.
8 egg yolks 100 gm caster sugar	In a stainless steel bowl, whisk until pale and thick. Then add cream mixture and combine well. Put over simmering water (without allowing base of bowl to touch the water) and cook until thickened. Strain, pour into small ramekins and put in a baking dish. Fill halfway up sides of the ramekins with boiling water and bake for 30 minutes or until just set. Remove and, when cool, refrigerate overnight.
50 gm caster sugar a blowtorch	Using a sieve, sprinkle a layer of sugar over top of each custard and caramelise with the blowtorch. Rest for 10 minutes then serve. Serves 4–6

'What would bistros have done without the Crème Brûlée? The first time I tasted this great dessert was in a bistro in Paris where they cracked the crust at the table and poured in a spoonful of Grand Marnier – delicious.'

Oeufs à la Neige with Passionfruit Anglaise & Orange Caramel
(Snow Eggs)

6 egg whites 200 gm sugar a few drops vanilla essence	To make snow eggs, beat egg whites until soft peaks form. Add sugar gradually, beating until stiff peaks form, then mix in vanilla. Shape into large 'eggs' using 2 tablespoons. Poach, without overcrowding, in just simmering water for 2 minutes. Turn over and poach for another 1–2 minutes until firm to the touch. Drain and cool on kitchen towels.
2 cups thickened cream seeds of ½ vanilla bean	Put in a pot, bring to the boil then remove from heat. Set aside for 30 minutes.
6 egg yolks 100 gm sugar pulp of 3–4 passionfruit	To make anglaise, whisk yolks and sugar with hand mixer until pale and thick. Bring cream back to boil and gradually add through a strainer, whisking continually. Cook over double boiler until mixture coats the back of a wooden spoon. Cool slightly then add passionfruit.
125 gm sugar 250 ml water grated zest & segments of 1 ½ oranges	Bring sugar and water to the boil in a heavy-bottomed pot. Cook, without stirring, until a deep caramel. Mix in zest and orange segments.
Grand Marnier	Carefully add a splash to caramel. To serve, put anglaise on plates, top with snow eggs and place orange segments around. Pour caramel over. Serves 4–6

Cam's Berry Pond

2 punnets raspberries ¼ cup caster sugar a splash of framboise (raspberry) liqueur	Blend until smooth then strain.
1 punnet strawberries, halved 1 punnet raspberries 1 punnet blueberries	Add to puree carefully and mix through. Share between large flat soup bowls.
Vanilla Bean Ice-cream, bought or homemade (page 259) 1 punnet redcurrants	Put 2 scoops of vanilla ice-cream in centre of each and scatter with redcurrants. Serves 6–8

Tarte aux Pommes
(French Apple Tart)

2–3 Granny Smiths, peeled & cored	Preheat oven to 200°C. Halve and cut into very thin slices.
1 sheet of puff pastry, bought or homemade (page 258)	Place on a baking tray and mark out a 1.5 cm border from edges all round. Then place apples in rows, overlapping slightly, leaving border clear.
soft brown sugar unsalted butter	Sprinkle generously with sugar and dot with butter.
1 egg ¼ cup milk	Beat together and brush on pastry border. Then bake until border is risen and pastry is golden brown.
whipped cream	Serve hot with whipped cream. Serves 2–4

Ed's Triple Chocolate Mousse Cake

dark cooking chocolate	Line the bottom of a 20 cm springform tin with baking paper. Melt some chocolate and pour a thin layer into base of tin and set.
280 gm dark cooking chocolate 115 gm unsalted butter 4 egg yolks 2 tsp instant coffee, dissolved in 2 tsp hot water	Melt chocolate and butter in microwave on 50 per cent for about 2 minutes. Then add egg yolks and coffee and whisk well.
4 egg whites 1/8 tsp cream of tartar 2 tbsp caster sugar	Beat egg whites and cream of tartar until stiff peaks form then, little by little, add sugar. Fold in 4 lots into chocolate mix. Pour into tin, smooth top and freeze.
280 gm milk chocolate 5 tsp instant coffee, dissolved in 1/4 cup hot water	Melt in microwave on 50 per cent for about 2 minutes. Whisk well and set aside to cool.
350 gm thickened cream	Whisk to stiff peaks. Fold into milk chocolate mix and pour onto set first layer. Return to freezer.
280 gm white chocolate 1/4 cup hot water	Melt in microwave on 50 per cent for about 2 minutes. Whisk well and set aside to cool.
350 gm thickened cream	Whisk to soft–medium peaks and fold into white chocolate mixture very, very carefully. When second layer is set, pour on top. Cover and freeze overnight.
a selection of fresh berries	Remove from freezer 30 minutes before needed, cut into wedges with a hot knife. Serve with berries.

Serves 10-12

'Ed Golombok, who died very young, was one of our talented pastry chefs.'

One of my restaurants, Fleurie, was famous for its comprehensive cheese selection, most of which was imported from France. I would, of course, love to take credit for the idea of making a feature of it, in the style of the great restaurants of Europe. But I have to admit I was inspired by Leon Massoni who always had a good selection of cheeses, all in perfect condition, which were placed strategically on a table just inside the front door of Tolarno. He invariably served the cheese himself, imparting much knowledge along the way (in a similar vein to Graham Ferguson who performed the same task at Fleurie). And, at a time when a cheese selection mostly revolved around canned camembert and Danish blue served straight from the fridge, he succeeded in making good cheese a definite feature of the Tolarno menu.

Mini Pavlovas with Fresh Fruit & Passionfruit Syrup

3 egg whites 190 gm caster sugar	Preheat oven to 140°C. Beat egg whites with a hand mixer to stiff peaks. Then add sugar, little by little, until thick and glossy.
2 tsp cornflour 1 tsp white vinegar ½ tsp vanilla extract	Add and mix in well using a stainless steel kitchen spoon.
oil spray baking paper	Lightly oil a baking tray, cover with baking paper and mound 4–6 spoonfuls of meringue on top. Slightly flatten top and bake for about 30 minutes or until crispy but not coloured. Remove and cool.
75 ml water 50 gm caster sugar pulp of 8–10 passionfruit	Heat water and sugar in a small pot until sugar is dissolved. Cool for 1–2 minutes then whisk in passionfruit. Allow syrup to cool completely.
whipped cream 3 kiwifruit, peeled & sliced 1 punnet strawberries, sliced 1 small banana, sliced icing sugar	Top pavlovas with whipped cream and then fruit. Pour over passionfruit syrup, then dust with icing sugar.

Serves 4–6

Cappuccino Soufflé

80 gm crushed coffee beans 2 cups milk	A day ahead, combine and bring to boil. Allow to cool and refrigerate overnight.
	Preheat oven to 180°C. Strain milk and put 350 ml into pot. Bring to boil.
50 gm unsalted butter 40 gm plain flour a pinch of salt	Melt butter in another pot, add flour and mix well. Cook over low heat for a few minutes, then add hot milk and salt and whisk vigorously. Continue to cook over low heat until thick, then cool.
4 egg yolks 50 gm caster sugar 75 ml Tia Maria	Add and mix in well.
4 egg whites	Beat until soft peaks form then carefully fold in with a stainless steel spoon. Fill soufflé dishes to two-thirds full and cook in oven for 15–20 minutes until firmish when touched.
icing sugar	Dust with icing sugar.

Serves 4

Clafoutis aux Pruneaux
(Prune Custard Pudding)

250 gm pitted prunes 1 cup hot black tea (such as English breakfast) ½ cup brandy	Soak prunes in tea for 30 minutes to plump. Then drain and toss with brandy.
4 eggs 100 gm sugar seeds of 1 vanilla bean a pinch of salt a splash of prune soaking liquid	Preheat oven to 180°C. Beat eggs and sugar until thick and pale and then add vanilla, salt and liquid.
100 gm plain flour 350 ml milk	Add flour, whisk well, and add milk, continuing to whisk. Put prunes in a gratin dish and pour batter over the top. Cook until golden brown and risen (40–60 minutes).
icing sugar thickened or clotted cream	Dust with icing sugar and serve with cream alongside. Serves 6–8

'Unless you are in training and need to develop your muscles, use a hand-held electric mixer.'

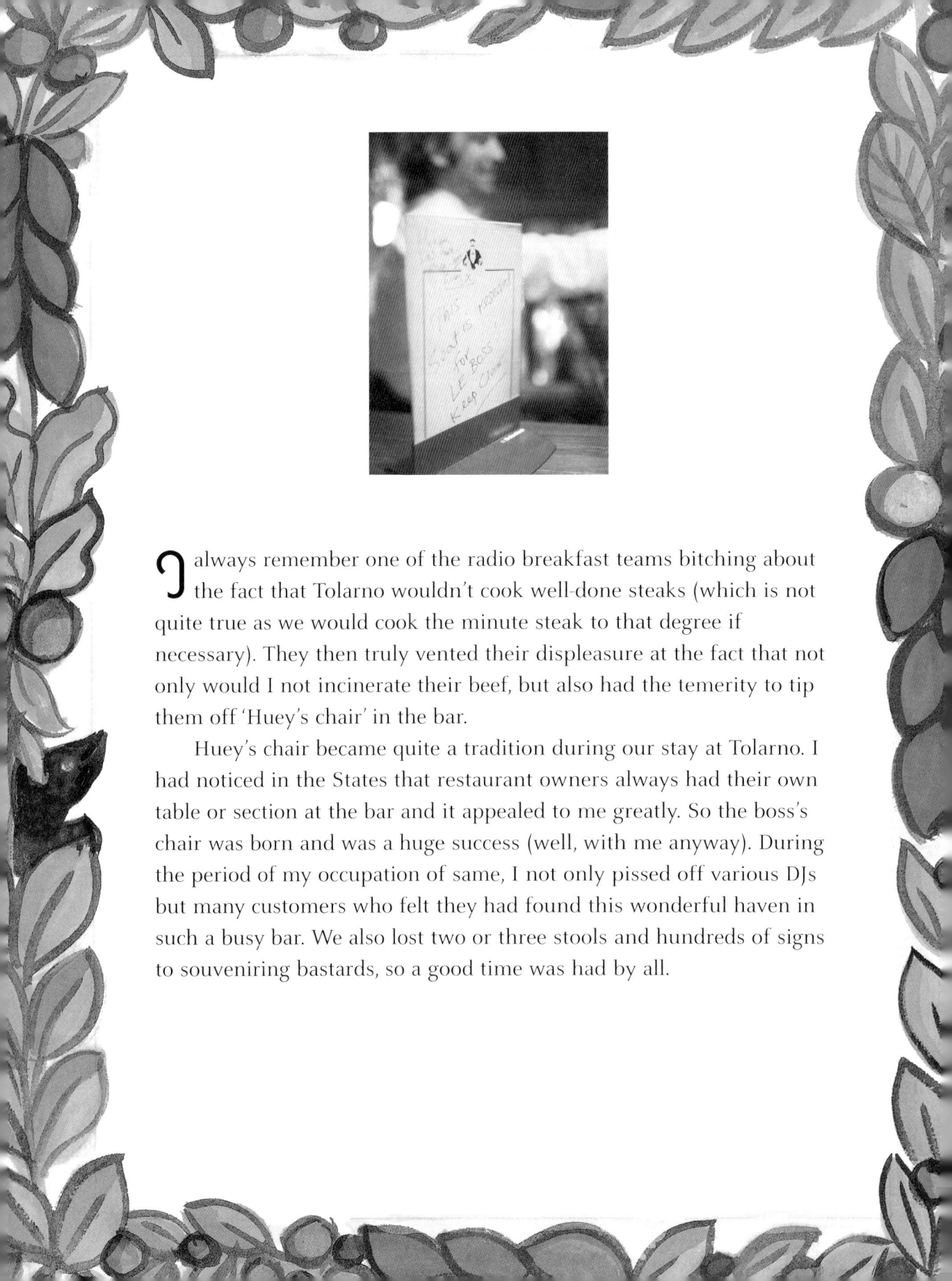

I always remember one of the radio breakfast teams bitching about the fact that Tolarno wouldn't cook well-done steaks (which is not quite true as we would cook the minute steak to that degree if necessary). They then truly vented their displeasure at the fact that not only would I not incinerate their beef, but also had the temerity to tip them off 'Huey's chair' in the bar.

Huey's chair became quite a tradition during our stay at Tolarno. I had noticed in the States that restaurant owners always had their own table or section at the bar and it appealed to me greatly. So the boss's chair was born and was a huge success (well, with me anyway). During the period of my occupation of same, I not only pissed off various DJs but many customers who felt they had found this wonderful haven in such a busy bar. We also lost two or three stools and hundreds of signs to souveniring bastards, so a good time was had by all.

Crêpes Suzette with Banana & Passionfruit Stuffing

2 large eggs 180 ml milk a pinch of sugar a pinch of sea salt 145 gm plain flour	To make crepes, whisk eggs, milk, sugar and salt. Then add flour and whisk until smooth (batter should be consistency of heavy cream). Set aside for 30 minutes.
200 gm butter 80 gm caster sugar	Put in a large heavy-bottomed pan and melt.
grated zest & juice of 4 oranges 4 tbsp Grand Marnier 3 bananas, sliced pulp of 4 passionfruit	Add and simmer for a few minutes.
a good knob of butter	Melt butter in a crepe pan and whisk into batter. Make 12 crepes. Place on plates then stuff with banana and passionfruit and roll up.
lightly whipped cream	Spoon juices over top and serve with cream on the side. Serves 4–6

'Not the most authentic version – Escoffier would most probably turn over in his grave.'

Tarte au Citron
(Lemon Tart)

2 cups fresh lemon juice 500 gm caster sugar	Preheat oven to 150°C. Combine, whisk well and set aside for 10 minutes.
2 cups eggs, whisked 2 cups thickened cream	Add, whisk well then strain three times. Refrigerate for 30 minutes. Gently warm in a pot to just above tepid, stirring continually. Pour carefully into a jug.
Blind-baked Tart Shell (page 52)	Place tart shell on a baking tray in oven and pour lemon mixture into it. Bake until centre is almost set (still a little wobbly – like jelly). Remove from oven, cool and refrigerate overnight.
caster sugar thickened cream or Vanilla Bean Ice-cream (page 259)	Sprinkle with sugar and, using a blowtorch, carefully caramelise surface. Serve with cream or ice-cream.

Serves 8–12

'Another Cameron Cox masterpiece.'

A Trio of Ice-creams with Fresh Fruit
Cherry Yoghurt Ice-cream

50 gm glace cherries a little natural yoghurt	Whiz up in a processor.
8 egg yolks 125 gm sugar	Whisk until pale and thick.
2 cups yoghurt ½ cup thickened cream	With a wooden spoon, add cherry mixture to yolks, little by little. Then carefully fold in yoghurt and cream, little by little,. Churn in an ice-cream machine, then put in freezer.

Jaffa Ice-cream

1 cup freshly squeezed orange juice	Boil in a pot until reduced by half. Set aside to cool.
125 gm sugar 90 ml water	Bring to boil in another pot.
4 egg yolks	Whisk in a bowl until pale, add sugar syrup and cook over simmering water until mixture coats the back of a wooden spoon.
1 ½ cups thickened cream 1 tbsp grated orange zest 1 tbsp Grand Marnier	Cool, mix in a bowl over ice, then add cream, zest and Grand Marnier. Stir in cooled orange juice.
50 gm dark cooking chocolate, chopped	Add, mix in and churn in an ice-cream machine, then put in freezer.

Rhubarb Ripple Ice-cream

120 gm sugar 80 ml water 6 egg yolks	Bring sugar and water to the boil then add to yolks. Whisk in a heatproof bowl over a pot of simmering water until doubled in volume.
1 cup thickened cream 1 vanilla bean, split	Put in a pot and bring to just below boiling point. Leave to stand for 15 minutes then remove vanilla bean, scraping seeds into cream. Add egg mixture and cool.
1 cup thickened cream	Add and churn in an ice-cream machine.
150 ml sweetened stewed rhubarb (should be sweeter than normal)	When ice-cream is ready, fold rhubarb through, then put in freezer.

To serve the ice-creams

A selection of fresh fruit (mango, kiwifruit, berries, pineapple, lychees and so on), prepared as necessary	Place a scoop of each ice-cream in centre of a large plate and arrange fruit neatly around the edges.
Passionfruit Syrup (page 238)	Drizzle over the fruit.

Serves 10 +

Poires à la Beaujolaise

3 cups Beaujolais ¾ cup caster sugar 1 cinnamon stick 1 whole clove 2 slices orange 2 slices lemon 5 black peppercorns	Put in a heavy-bottomed pot and simmer for 10 minutes.
6 large pears, peeled with stems intact	Add and cook until tender. Cool in syrup.
¾ cup crème de cassis (blackcurrant liqueur)	Stir into cooled syrup.
crème fraiche or clotted cream	Serve with a generous amount of the syrup and a good dollop of crème fraiche or clotted cream. Serves 6

'A recipe from the master, Paul Bocuse.'

Bande au Poires
(Poached Pear Tart)

3 cups red wine 125 gm sugar juice of 2 lemons 1 cinnamon stick 6 firm pears, peeled, cored & halved	Put wine, sugar, juice and cinnamon stick into a heavy-bottomed pot. Bring to boil and add pears. Reduce to simmer and poach gently until pears are tender. Remove pears and drain well, removing poaching syrup.
2 tbsp redcurrant jelly	Add to 1–2 cups of the poaching liquid and reduce over high heat to a glaze. Taste, adding more jelly or poaching liquid as required. Set aside.
puff pastry, bought or homemade (page 258) egg wash (1 egg beaten with ¼ cup milk)	Preheat oven to 200°C. Roll pastry into a large rectangle. Cut into shape about 2–3 cm more than is needed to hold all the pears in one layer. Place on a baking tray. Cut strips 2 cm wide to go around edges. Brush edges with egg wash and press pastry strips on firmly. Brush top of these additions, before pricking base all over with a fork. Cook in oven until sides have risen, then lower temperature to 160 degrees and allow centre to cook. Cool on a rack.
Crème Pâtissière (page 259) whipped cream or Vanilla Bean Ice-cream, bought or homemade (page 259)	Spread centre with pastry cream, top with pears and brush generously with redcurrant glaze. Serve with cream or ice-cream. Serves 6–8

What they said about Tolarno

People living south and east of Melbourne are the diners-out, those living north and west of the city are the stay-at-homes, says restaurateur Georges Mora … who came here to live in 1951 [and] has been studying our eating habits in the six years since he opened a French restaurant in East Melbourne. Mr Mora has just opened a new French bistro in Fitzroy St, St Kilda, serving only Parisian style food (so there'll be no strong garlic flavour or aroma). 'I've always felt the street had a French atmosphere, which made me want to open this type of restaurant there.'

The Herald, 28 November 1964

Leon Massoni, of the famous restaurant family which used to own Florentino, has built the Tolarno into one of Melbourne's most pleasant places. Madly busy, very informal and extraordinarily good value, it is a French-style bistro of individuality and charm. Why are they open seven days a week? 'Because we're mad,' says Leon. If so, it's a sort of lunacy I wish would catch on.

Eating Out in Melbourne 1979, Peter Smark & Anne Latreille, Angus & Robertson Publishers, Australia, 1979

Leon Massoni has a passion for restaurants and yachts. In both pursuits he runs a tight ship … 'I could not bear to run an unsuccessful place,' says Leon, as he looks around the packed room at Tolarno. If everything is not just perfect, he is unhappy and restless.

Chef's Choice, Eric Page, The Herald and Weekly Times, Melbourne, 1985

They said it brought respectability to Fitzroy Street. Respectability aside, Tolarno Bistro is probably better known as one of Melbourne's best eating houses. Set in the heart of St Kilda, the bistro is as much part of the area as Leo's, the Esplanade on Sundays and Luna Park.

The Herald, 26 March 1987

[Tolarno Bar and Bistro] is seriously good French food blended with the flavours of North Africa and Asia despite the modest moniker. Iain Hewitson has reworked this long-established 60s bistro, where many Melburnians first dipped into onion soup, and has taken it to the culinary frontline.

Courvoissier's Book of the Best, edited by Loyd Grossman, Random House UK, 1996

There probably aren't enough restaurants in Melbourne that have the word 'arse' on their menu. The offending word is, of course, used in the context of celebrity chef Iain Hewitson's Kick-Arse sauce, but it does separate Tolarno from the crowd. And it has always been that way. Tolarno sticks to its knitting, revels in its irreverence, cooks really tasty food and cares about its customers.

The Age Good Food Guide, 2002

End of an era

Melbourne's friendliest bar, Tolarno Bar and Bistro, will call 'last drinks' for the last time tomorrow, another victim of rising rents and the gentrification of the inner suburbs ... The appeal of a unique business has as much to do with the X factor, created by passionate staff and the characters who prop up the bar. Tolarno harks back to the days when a little bit of old-fashioned service went a long way.

The Age, 26 May 2006

For me, there are so many memories here. So many ghosts. Not just my paintings but so much of my life. This whole place is a work of art and nothing should be allowed to change. I will never forget the day Georges came home and told us he'd bought the Tolarno Hotel ... lots of rooms, lots of atmosphere, lots of magic. We had a wonderful life here.

Mirka Mora, 27 May 2006

To local foodies, and to those in tune with Melbourne's glorious culinary past, this will be remembered, sadly, as the day the music died. Because tonight, the doors of Tolarno Bar and Bistro in Fitzroy Street will open, and close, for the last time. And when telly chef, restaurateur and passionate St Kilda resident Iain Hewitson leaves Tolarno in the early hours of tomorrow, the name and spirit of the place, and the hoards of tearful regulars, will leave with him ... Anguish over the closure relates not to the loss of the amenity ... Rather, it is to do with the loss of our history ...

Herald Sun, 27 May 2006

⬇ Huey, Mirka and Leon, 26 May 2006

Chicken Stock
Vegetable Stock
Beef Stock
Fish Stock
Demi-glaze
Homemade Mayonnaise
Aïoli
Dijon Mustard Aïoli
Mustard Vinaigrette
Tartare Sauce
Harissa
Basil Pistou
Couscous
Mornay Sauce
Beetroot Chutney
Tomato Chutney
Pâte Feuilletée
Crème Pâtissière
Vanilla Bean Ice-cream

BASICS

'Traditional Bistro Food is the essence of French Country Cooking – honest, fresh and satisfying food prepared by cooks not Michelin trained chefs. It's not expensive, it's not complicated and it never goes out of fashion. Bistro food is real food for real people.'
Laura Washburn
Bistro, 2003

Chicken Stock
Makes 3–4 litres

1 boiling fowl
2 kg chicken carcasses
2 onions, chopped
2 carrots, washed & chopped
2 leeks, washed & chopped
1 celery stalk, washed & copped
5 litres cold water
3 fresh thyme sprigs
1 slice of lemon
1 bay leaf
4 whole black peppercorns

Section the fowl and chop the carcasses. Put in a stockpot along with everything else. Bring to the boil and simmer very, very gently for 3 hours, skimming frequently and topping up with more water if chicken becomes exposed. DO NOT STIR. Strain, cool and refrigerate overnight. Next day, remove fat from the surface.

Vegetable Stock
Makes 2–3 litres

2 leeks, washed & coarsely chopped
2 onions, coarsely chopped
6 tomatoes, washed & coarsely chopped
4 garlic cloves
60 g fresh herbs
2 lemons, sliced
4 litres cold water
2 star anise
2 good slurps white wine
sea salt & freshly ground pepper

Put everything in a large pot and rapidly boil for 20 minutes. Cool, then strain through muslin and refrigerate.

Beef Stock
Makes 3 litres

4 kg veal or small beef bones, including knuckles & marrow bones
1 kg beef brisket
100 gm ghee
100 gm honey
3 large carrots, unpeeled & chopped
4 leeks, washed & chopped
2 celery stalks, chopped
a handful of mushroom peelings & stalks
6 garlic cloves, chopped
1 bottle dry white wine
2 large onions, skin on & halved
parsley stalks
2 bay leaves
12 whole black peppercorns
2 x 800 gm cans diced tomatoes, drained

Preheat oven to 200°C.

Coarsely chop brisket and put in a large roasting pan with bones. Melt ghee and honey, brush all over and cook in oven until lightly browned. Then put in a stock pot.

Add vegetables to the roasting pan and sauté until lightly brown. Then add wine and reduce until almost evaporated. Add to stock pot.

Cook onions, skin-side down, until dark brown. Then add to pot along with cold water to about 10 cm above contents. Bring to boil then simmer very gently, regularly skimming for 30 minutes.

Add to pot and simmer for 4–5 hours, adding more water if bones become exposed. Strain, cool and refrigerate overnight. Next day, remove the layer of fat.

Fish Stock
Makes 2 litres

2 kg fish bones, including heads
2 tbsp olive oil
2 onions, roughly chopped
1 celery stalk, chopped
1 medium carrot, chopped
2 leeks, well washed & chopped
2 garlic cloves, chopped
10 black peppercorns
2 bay leaves
4 parsley stalks
2.5 litres of water
2 cups dry white wine

Thoroughly wash bones, removing all traces of blood. Remove eyes and gills and wash heads well. Chop bones into 10cm lengths.

Heat oil in a large heavy-bottomed pot, add vegetables and sauté gently for 5 minutes. Add bones, peppercorns, bay leaves and parsley and toss for a few more minutes.

Add water and wine and water and bring to boil. Simmer for 20 minutes, skimming frequently. Turn off and stand for 20 minutes, before straining.

'When making stocks, do not peel the vegies.'

Demi-glaze
Makes about 1 litre

vegetable oil
1 kg veal bones (including knuckle), chopped into small pieces by your butcher
500 gm lean stewing steak, cut into large cubes
4 garlic cloves, crushed
3 medium carrots, chopped
3 medium onions, chopped
2 celery stalks, chopped
2 tbsp tomato paste
2 cups red wine
4 litres veal or beef stock, bought (low salt) or homemade (page xx)
a few sprigs of fresh thyme
a few stalks of fresh parsley
2 bay leaves

Preheat oven to 210°C.

Drizzle bones and meat with oil and toss to coat. Bake in oven until golden, turning regularly.

Add garlic, vegetables and tomato paste, mix well and return to oven to colour a little. Then put in a large stockpot.

Add wine, stock and herbs and bring to simmer. Cook very gently, skimming as needed, for 4–5 hours. Then strain into a fresh pot and cook down until glaze is formed. Will keep, covered, in the fridge for up to two weeks or can be frozen in ice cube containers.

'An essential part of restaurant cooking, a good slurp of demi adds that touch of class to any grill or roast.'

BASICS

Homemade Mayonnaise
Makes 2 cups

2 large eggs
2 egg yolks
1 tbsp Dijon mustard
2 pinches sea salt
2 cups vegetable oil
lemon juice
freshly ground pepper

Put eggs, yolks, mustard and salt in a food processor and whiz up for 1 minute. Add oil through feeder tube, little by little, until incorporated. Then add lemon juice and pepper to taste.

Aïoli
Makes 1 cup

1 cup bought or homemade mayonnaise (page xx)
1 tsp Dijon mustard
3 garlic cloves, crushed
a squeeze of fresh lemon juice

Mix all ingredients together.

Dijon Mustard Aïoli

As above, using 1 tbsp Dijon mustard

Mix all ingredients together.

Mustard Vinaigrette
Makes about 1 1/2 cups

2 tbsp Dijon mustard
1 garlic clove, crushed
300 ml vegetable oil
50 ml white wine vinegar
sea salt & freshly ground pepper

Whisk mustard and garlic for 1 minute. Add oil, little by little, whisking continually. Whisk in vinegar and season to taste.

Tartare Sauce
Makes 1 cup

1 cup bought or homemade mayonnaise (page 256)
1 tbsp drained & chopped capers
2 cornichons (baby gherkins), finely chopped
2 tbsp chopped fresh parsley
1 tbsp finely chopped red onion

Mix all ingredients together.

Harissa
Makes about 1/2 cup

4 tbsp coriander seeds
2 tbsp cumin seeds
6 tbsp olive oil
8 fresh chillies, chopped
4 garlic cloves, crushed
a good pinch of sea salt

Toast seeds in a hot dry pan for a few minutes over moderate heat. Put in a processor or mortar. Add oil, chillies, garlic and salt and blend or grind with pestle. This will keep for a month in the refrigerator.

Basil Pistou
Makes about 1 cup

8 large garlic cloves
24 fresh basil leaves
up to 1 cup olive oil
8 tbsp freshly grated parmesan
sea salt & freshly ground pepper

Whiz garlic and basil in a processor, then add oil, little by little, through feeder tube. Remove to a bowl and mix in the parmesan. Season to taste.

'Pistou is, of course, the Provençal version of pesto.'

Couscous
Serves 4–6

1 cup fresh orange juice
1 tsp ground cinnamon
2 tbsp olive oil
1 cup couscous
2 tbsp raisins
a good dollop of soft unsalted butter
2 tbsp chopped fresh coriander

Bring juice, cinnamon and oil to boil in a small pot. Place couscous and raisins in a bowl and pour liquid over the top. Cover with plastic wrap and leave for 5 minutes. Add butter and coriander and fluff with a fork.

Mornay Sauce
Makes 3–4 cups

3 tbsp butter
3 tbsp plain flour
3 cups hot milk
a good handful of grated tasty cheese
a splash of cream
sea salt & freshly ground black pepper

Put butter in a heavy-bottomed pot and melt. Add flour, mix well and cook over low heat for a few minutes. Then add milk, all at once, and whisk vigorously. Cook until thick. Add cheese, cream and seasoning and cook until cheese has melted, adding more milk if too thick.

Beetroot Chutney

500 gm beetroot
250 gm onions, roughly chopped.
1 cup vinegar
1 cup sugar
½ tbsp rock salt
½ tbsp mustard seeds
½ tsp coriander seeds
½ tsp allspice berries, crushed
freshly ground pepper

Cook beetroot until tender. When cool enough to handle, peel and chop.

Put rest of ingredients into a pot along with beetroot and gently simmer for 30-40 minutes until thick. Cool. Will keep for a month or two in the refrigerator, or longer if put into sterilised jars.

Tomato Chutney

3 kg tomatoes
1 kg onions, roughly chopped
3 heaped tsp sea salt
1 kg white sugar
white vinegar
1 tbsp curry powder
¼ tbsp cayenne pepper
1 tbsp Dijon mustard
2 heaped tbsp sambal oelek

Put vegetables in a large colander over a bowl and toss salt through. Refrigerate for 24 hours.

Put drained tomato mix in a large pot. Add sugar and almost cover with vinegar. Bring to the boil. Add rest of ingredients and simmer until fragrant and thick, adding a little more water if needed. Will keep for a month or two in the refrigerator, or longer if put into sterilised jars.

Pâte Feuilletée (Puff Pastry)
Makes 1 kg

350 gm plain flour
50 gm cold butter, cubed
1 egg yolk
180 ml water
10 gm sea salt
400 gm slightly softened butter
150 gm plain flour

Mix flour and butter with your fingertips until mixture resembles breadcrumbs.

Combine egg yolk, water and salt, then add to flour and butter and mix until a dough is formed. Roll out onto a floured work surface to form a 1-cm thick rectangle.

In another bowl mix softened butter and flour together. Spread evenly on top of dough. Fold up, as you would an envelope, wrap in plastic wrap and refrigerate for 20 minutes. Remove, turn pastry one turn to the right then roll out to 1-cm thick. Fold as before and refrigerate for another 20 minutes. Repeat the turning-rolling-folding process twice more, turning to the right each time. Turn and roll one last time, then fold the left third to the centre, then the right third over it. Rest pastry for at least 1 hour before using.

'While I'm quite a fan of frozen puff pastry sheets, the homemade version is not really difficult. So, if you have the time, please give it a shot. The only real trick is to make sure that the softened butter is not too soft as it will ooze out if that's the case.'

Crème Pâtissière (Pastry Cream)

Makes 2–3 cups

6 egg yolks
170 gm sugar
70 gm flour
450 ml hot milk
unsalted butter
orange liqueur (such as Cointreau)
1/2 cup thickened cream, lightly whipped

Beat egg yolks and sugar with a hand mixer until pale and thick. Add flour, mixing well, then mix in hot milk. Put in a heavy-bottomed pot and whisk over medium heat until thickened. Add a few dobs of butter and a little liqueur to taste. Cool and fold in cream.

Vanilla Bean Ice-cream

Serves 4–6

6 egg yolks
250 gm caster sugar
1 cup milk
seeds of 1 vanilla bean
1 cup thickened cream

Beat egg yolks and sugar in a heatproof bowl with a hand-held electric mixer, until pale and thick.˙

Put milk and vanilla bean in a pot and bring to just below boiling point. Combine with egg yolks and sugar and cook over simmering water until the custard coats the back of a wooden spoon. Cool over ice. Add cream and churn in an ice-cream machine. Place in freezer.

'To remove seeds from the vanilla bean, cut bean in half lengthways then place on bench, cut-side up, and scrape seeds out with the tip of a sharp knife.'

Index

A

Aïoli 256
    Dijon Mustard Aïoli 256
Anchovy & Cheese Straws 22
apples
    Black Pudding with Apples 143
    French Apple Tart 234
    Pork Fillet with Calvados & Glazed Apples 176
Artichauts Hollandaise 53
Asparagus with Double Peeled Broad Beans, Olive Oil, Balsamic & Parmesan 55

B

bacon
    Chicken in a Pot with Bacon, Onions & Mushrooms 92
    Curly Endive Salad with Bacon & Poached Egg 193
    French Bacon & Beans 177
    Fresh Peas with Lettuce, Onion & Bacon 203
    Liver, Spinach & Bacon Salad with Mustard Vinaigrette 198
The Baker's Potatoes 210
bananas
    Crêpes Suzette with Banana & Passionfruit Stuffing 243
Bande au Poires 249
Le Bar Burger 174
Barley & Pumpkin Pilaf 141
basil
    Basil Pistou 257
    A Provençal Vegetable Soup with Basil 70
BBQ Leeks with a Piquant Sauce 60
beans
    Asparagus with Double Peeled Broad Beans, Olive Oil, Balsamic & Parmesan 55
    French Bacon & Beans 177
Béarnaise Sauce 170
beef
    Beef Stock 254
    Fillet Steak with Green Peppercorn Sauce 166
    Minute Steak with Café de Paris Butter 168
    Peppered Porterhouse Salad 189
    Poached Fillet of Beef on a String 169
    Provençal Beef Stew 164
    Roasted Fillet of Beef with Béarnaise Sauce 170
    Shepherd's Pie 135
    Steak Tartare with Parmesan & Garlic Toasts 165
    The Tolarno Burger 174
Beetroot Chutney 257

berries
    Cam's Berry Pond 234
    Peach Melba 227
Black Pudding with Apples 143
Blanquette de Veau à l'Ancienne 137
blini
    Potato Blini with Smoked Salmon & Salmon Caviar 65
Blue Swimmer Crabs in the Bouillabaisse Style 110
Boudin Noir aux Pommes 143
bouillabaisse
    Blue Swimmer Crabs in the Bouillabaisse Style 110
Bouillabaisse de Crabe 110
Bourride 105
brains
    Brain, Yabbie & Sweetbread Stew 145
    Lambs' Brains with Brown Butter 144
Braised Chicken with Capsicum, Pancetta & Tomato 93
Braised Duck in a Casserole 101
Braised Lamb with Vegetables 130
bread
    Dill & Cottage Cheese Bread 38
    Garlic Bread 34
    Parmesan & Garlic Toasts 165
    Wholemeal Bread 35
Brochettes d'Agneau 128
Brochettes de Foie de Canard 100
brussels sprouts
    Creamed Brussels Sprouts 205
burger
    The Tolarno Burger 174
butters
    Beurre Maître d'Hôtel 116
    Café de Paris Butter 168
    Garlic Butter 48
    Lemon Butter 125
    Lemon & Caper Butter 117

C

cabbage
    Lentil & Cabbage Stew 178
    Sauerkraut in the Style of Alsace 181
cakes
    Ed's Triple Chocolate Mousse Cake 235
Cam's Berry Pond 234
Caneton à l'Orange 97
Caneton en Casserole 101
capers
    Lemon & Caper Butter 117
Cappuccino Soufflé 239
capsicum
    Braised Chicken with Capsicum, Pancetta & Tomato 93
    Tuna with a Spiced Tomato, Capsicum & Potato Stew 122

caramel
    Cream Caramel 228
    Orange Caramel 232
Carré d'Agneau Persillé 129
carrots
    Cream of Carrot Soup 68
casserole
    Braised Duck in a Casserole 101
Celery Root with a Piquant Mayonnaise 18
Cervelles d'Agneau Grenobloise 144
Champignons et Oignons à la Grecque 18
Châteaubriand Sauce Béarnaise 170
cheese
    Anchovy & Cheese Straws 22
    Cheese Gratinéed French Onion Soup 73
    Cheese Gratinéed Lobster in Mustard Cream 109
    Cheese Gratinéed Seafood Crepes 112
    A Creamy, Cheesy Potato Gratin 212
    Dill & Cottage Cheese Bread 38
    Leek & Cheese Tart 52
    Macaroni & Corn Cheese 56
    Parmesan & Garlic Toasts 165
    Parmesan-crumbed Veal with Dubonnet & Orange 136
    Slow-roasted Tomatoes on Sourdough with Feta 58
    Twice Baked Cheese Soufflés 61
The Chef's Pork, Veal & Liver Terrine 33
Cherry Yoghurt Ice-cream 246
chicken
    Braised Chicken with Capsicum, Pancetta & Tomato 93
    Chicken in a Pot with Bacon, Onions & Mushrooms 92
    Chicken in Red Wine 90
    Chicken Stock 254
    Devilled Chicken 89
    Flemish Stewed Chicken 88
    Sautéed Chicken with Tarragon 94
Chilled Leek & Potato Soup 72
chips
    The Perfect Chips 211
    Polenta Chips 23
chocolate
    Chocolate Mousse 226
    Ed's Triple Chocolate Mousse Cake 235
    Jaffa Ice-cream 246
Choucroûte Garnie 181
Choux de Bruxelles à la Crème 205
Choux Pastry Cake Stuffed with Pastry Cream & Fresh Fruit 230
chutney
    Beetroot Chutney 257
    Tomato Chutney 258
Clafoutis aux Pruneaux 241

Classic Sautéed Potatoes 212
coffee
    Cappuccino Soufflé 239
Confit de Caneton 96
Coq au Vin 90
Coquilles St Jacques à la Provençale 104
corn
    Macaroni & Corn Cheese 56
Côte de Porc Charcutière 182
couscous 98, 257
crab
    Blue Swimmer Crabs in the Bouillabaisse Style 110
Cream Caramel 228
Cream of Carrot Soup 68
Creamed Brussels Sprouts 205
Creamed Spinach 200
creams
    Crème Pâtissière 15
    Passionfruit Anglaise 232
    Pastry Cream 15
Creamy Mash 209
A Creamy, Cheesy Potato Gratin 212
Crème Brûlée 231
Crème Crécy 68
Crème Pâtissière 15
Crème Renversée au Caramel 228
Crème Vichyssoise Glacée 72
crepes
    Cheese Gratinéed Seafood Crepes 112
    Crêpes Suzette with Banana & Passionfruit Stuffing 243
Crevettes à l'Ail 113
Crispy Skinned Salmon with a Tomato, Fresh Herb & Lemon Oil 119
Crumbed Mushrooms 26
Curly Endive Salad with Bacon & Poached Egg 193
custard
    Glazed English Custard Cream 231
    Passionfruit Anglaise 232
    Prune Custard Pudding 241

D

Daube de Boeuf à la Provençale 164
Demi-glaze 255
Devilled Chicken 89
Devilled Lambs' Kidneys 146
Dijon Mustard Aïoli 9
Dill & Cottage Cheese Bread 38
duck
    Braised Duck in a Casserole 101
    Duck Cooked in its Own Fat 96
    Duck Liver Skewers 100
    Duck with Orange Sauce 97
    Tagine of Duck Confit, Lamb Kefta & Merguez Sausage in Harissa Broth 98

E

Ed's Triple Chocolate Mousse Cake 235
eggs
    Curly Endive Salad with Bacon & Poached Egg 193
    Eggs on a Plate with Spinach 64
    Oeufs à la Neige with Passionfruit Anglaise & Orange Caramel 232
    A Provençal Vegetable Stew with a Poached Egg 66
Eggplant, Onion & Tomato Gratin 206
Entrecôte Minute et Beurre Café de Paris 168
Épinards à la Crème 200
Escalopes de Veau au Citron 133
Escargots à la Bourguignonne 48

F

The Farmer's Vegetable Soup 76
Filet de Boeuf à la Ficelle 169
Filet de Merlan Meunière 125
Filet de Porc Vallée d'Auge 176
Fillet Steak with Green Peppercorn Sauce 166
fish
    Crispy Skinned Salmon with a Tomato, Fresh Herb & Lemon Oil 119
    Fish 'n' Chips 120
    Fish Stock 255
    House Salted Fish Cakes with Dijon Mustard Aïoli 57
    John Dory with Lemon & Caper Butter 117
    A Salad in the Style of Nice with Fresh Tuna 190
    Snapper with Pistou Mash, Parmesan & Brown Butter 124
    Trout with Almonds 121
    Tuna with a Spiced Tomato, Capsicum & Potato Stew 122
    Whiting Fillets with Lemon Butter 125
    see also smoked salmon
Flamiche aux Poireaux 52
Flemish Stewed Chicken 88
French Apple Tart 234
French Bacon & Beans 177
Fresh Peas with Lettuce, Onion & Bacon 203
Freshly Shucked Oysters with Spicy Sausages 20
Fricassée de Poulet 'Waterzooi' 88

G

Galette de Poisson Salé avec Aïoli 57
Garbure 69
garlic
    Garlic Bread 34
    Garlic Butter 48
    Garlic Prawns 113
    Parmesan & Garlic Toasts 165
Gigot d'Agneau Rôti à la Provençale 132
Glazed English Custard Cream 231
Globe Artichokes with Hollandaise Sauce 53
Gratin Dauphinois 212
Gratin de Macaroni et Maïs 56
Gratinéed Tomatoes 208
Green Peppercorn Sauce 166

H

Hachis Parmentier 135
Harissa 256
A Hearty Winter Soup from the Basque Region 69
herbs
    Sautéed Chicken with Tarragon 94
    Herb Mayonnaise 148
    Tomato, Fresh Herb & Lemon Oil 119
Homard à la Parisienne 109
Homemade Mayonnaise 256
Home-style Veal Shanks 138
House Liver Pâté 30
House Salted Fish Cakes with Dijon Mustard Aïoli 57
Huîtres et Saucisses 20

I

ice-cream
    Cherry Yoghurt Ice-cream 246
    Jaffa Ice-cream 246
    Rhubarb Ripple Ice-cream 247

J

Jarret de Veau à la Menagère 138
Jellied Oxtail Terrine 27
John Dory with Lemon & Caper Butter 117

K

Kangaroo with Barley & Pumpkin Pilaf and a Black Pepper & Lemon-spiked Sauce 141
kebabs
    Duck Liver Skewers 100
    Lamb & Lambs' Kidneys on Skewers 128
kidneys
    Devilled Lambs' Kidneys 146
    Lamb & Lambs' Kidneys on Skewers 128

L

lamb
    Braised Lamb with Vegetables 130
    Devilled Lambs' Kidneys 146
    Lambs' Brains with Brown Butter 144
    Lamb & Lambs' Kidneys on Skewers 128
    Rack of Lamb with Garlic & Herb Crumbs 129
    Roast Leg of Lamb with the Flavours of Provence 132
    Shepherd's Pie 135
    Tagine of Duck Confit, Lamb Kefta & Merguez Sausage in Harissa Broth 98

Langue de Boeuf Grillée Sauce Rémoulade 148
leeks
   BBQ Leeks with a Piquant Sauce 60
   Chilled Leek & Potato Soup 72
   Leek & Cheese Tart 52
lemon
   Black Pepper & Lemon-spiked Sauce 141
   Lemon Butter 125
   Lemon & Caper Butter 117
   Lemon Tart 244
   Tomato, Fresh Herb & Lemon Oil 119
Lentil & Cabbage Stew 178
Les Crêpes aux Fruits de Mer 112
lettuce
   Fresh Peas with Lettuce, Onion & Bacon 203
liver
   Liver, Spinach & Bacon Salad with Mustard Vinaigrette 198
   see also pâté; terrines
lobster
   Cheese Gratinéed Lobster in Mustard Cream 109
   Lobster Soufflé 49
   Lobster & Spinach Quenelles with Lobster Sauce 114–15

M
Macaroni & Corn Cheese 56
mashes
   Creamy Mash 209
   Parsnip Mash 209
   Pistou Mash 124
   Roasted Sweet Potato Mash 204
mayonnaise
   Aïoli 256
   Dijon Mustard Aïoli 256
   Herb Mayonnaise 148
   Homemade Mayonnaise 256
   Piquant Mayonnaise 18
Mini Pavlovas with Fresh Fruit & Passionfruit Syrup 238
Minute Steak with Café de Paris Butter 168
Moreton Bay bugs
   Roasted Moreton Bay Bugs with Beurre Maître d'Hôtel 116
Mornay Sauce 257
Moules à la Portugaise 108
Moules Marinière 106
mousses
   Chocolate Mousse 226
Mousse au Chocolat 226
mushrooms
   Chicken in a Pot with Bacon, Onions & Mushrooms 92
   Crumbed Mushrooms 26
   Mushrooms & Onions Poached in a Greek Broth 18
   White Veal Stew with Onions & Mushrooms 137
Mussels in a White Wine Broth 106
Mussels in the Portuguese Style 108
mustard
   Dijon Mustard Aïoli 9
   Mustard Cream 109
   Mustard Vinaigrette 256

N
Navarin d'Agneau Printanier 130

O
Oeufs à la Neige with Passionfruit Anglaise & Orange Caramel (Snow Eggs) 232
Oeufs Sur le Plat 'Florentine' 64
offal
   Black Pudding with Apples 143
   Brain, Yabbie & Sweetbread Stew 145
   Devilled Lambs' Kidneys 146
   Lambs' Brains with Brown Butter 144
   Lamb & Lambs' Kidneys on Skewers 128
   Liver, Spinach & Bacon Salad with Mustard Vinaigrette 198
   Ox Tongue with Herb Mayonnaise 148
   Tongue, Pork & Spinach Terrine 28
   Tripe & Onions in the Style of Lyon 149
onions
   Cheese Gratinéed French Onion Soup 73
   Chicken in a Pot with Bacon, Onions & Mushrooms 92
   Eggplant, Onion & Tomato Gratin 206
   Fresh Peas with Lettuce, Onion & Bacon 203
   Mushrooms & Onions Poached in a Greek Broth 18
   Sautéed Potatoes with Onions 213
   Slow-roasted Onions With Olive Oil & Wine Vinegar 204
   Tripe & Onions in the Style of Lyon 149
   White Veal Stew with Onions & Mushrooms 137
oranges
   Crêpes Suzette with Banana & Passionfruit Stuffing 243
   Jaffa Ice-cream 246
   Orange Caramel 232
   Orange Sauce 97
   Parmesan-crumbed Veal with Dubonnet & Orange 136
Ox Tongue with Herb Mayonnaise 148
oxtail
   Jellied Oxtail Terrine 27
oysters
   Freshly Shucked Oysters with Spicy Sausages 20

P
Pain Complet 35
Paris Brest 230
Parmesan-crumbed Veal with Dubonnet & Orange 136
Parsnip Mash 209
passionfruit
   Crêpes Suzette with Banana & Passionfruit Stuffing 243
   Passionfruit Anglaise 232
   Passionfruit Syrup 238
pasta
   Macaroni & Corn Cheese 56
pastry
   Choux Pastry 230
   Puff Pastry 258
   Shortcrust Pastry 52
Pastry Cream 15
pastries
   Anchovy & Cheese Straws 22
   Choux Pastry Cake Stuffed with Pastry Cream & Fresh Fruit 230
   see also tarts
pâté
   House Liver Pâté 30
   Slow-cooked Shredded Pork Pâté in its own fat 31
Pâté de Foie Maison 30
Pâte Feuilletée 14
pavlovas
   Mini Pavlovas with Fresh Fruit & Passionfruit Syrup 238
Peach Melba 227
pears
   Poached Pear Tart 249
   Poires à la Beaujolaise 248
peas
   Fresh Peas with Lettuce, Onion & Bacon 203
   Snow Pea Soup with a Splash of Champagne 73
Pêche Melba 227
Peppered Porterhouse Salad 189
The Perfect Chips 211
Petits Pois à la Française 203
pie
   Shepherd's Pie 135
pilaf
   Barley & Pumpkin Pilaf 141
Pissaladière 36
Pistachio Sausage & Potato Salad 192
pistou
   Basil Pistou 257
pizza
   A Provençal Pizza 36
Poached Fillet of Beef on a String 169
Poached Pear Tart 249
Poireaux Grillé et Sauce Gribiche 60
Poires à la Beaujolaise 248
Polenta Chips 23
Pommes Boulangère 210
Pommes Sautées 212
Pommes Sautées à la Lyonnaise 213

pork
- The Chef's Pork, Veal & Liver Terrine 33
- The Pork Butcher's Chops 182
- Pork Fillet with Calvados & Glazed Apples 176
- Slow-cooked Shredded Pork Pâté in its Own Fat 31
- Tongue, Pork & Spinach Terrine 28

potatoes
- The Baker's Potatoes 210
- Chilled Leek & Potato Soup 72
- Classic Sautéed Potatoes 212
- A Creamy, Cheesy Potato Gratin 212
- Creamy Mash 209
- The Perfect Chips 211
- Pistachio Sausage & Potato Salad 192
- Pistou Mash 124
- Potato Blini with Smoked Salmon & Salmon Caviar 65
- A Salad in the Style of Lyon 188
- Sautéed Potatoes with Onions 213
- Shepherd's Pie 135
- Spiced Tomato, Capsicum & Potato Stew 122

Potted Smoked Salmon 25
Poulet Basquaise 93
Poulet en Cocotte Bonne Femme 92
Poulet Grillé à la Diable 89
Poulet Sauté a l'Estragon 94

prawns
- Garlic Prawns 113
- Prawn Cocktail 50

Provençal Beef Stew 164
A Provençal Pizza 36
A Provençal Vegetable Soup with Basil 70
A Provençal Vegetable Stew with a Poached Egg 66
Prune Custard Pudding 241
Puff Pastry 258

pumpkin
- Barley & Pumpkin Pilaf 141

Purée de Panais 209

Q

quenelles
- Lobster & Spinach Quenelles with Lobster Sauce 114–15

Quenelles de Langouste aux Épinards et Sauce Rouge 114–15

R

Rack of Lamb with Garlic & Herb Crumbs 129
Ragoût de Lucullus 145
Ratatouille Niçoise et Oeufs Pochés 66
Rhubarb Ripple Ice-cream 247
Rillettes de Porc 31
Roast Leg of Lamb with the Flavours of Provence 132
Roasted Fillet of Beef with Béarnaise Sauce 170
Roasted Moreton Bay Bugs with Beurre Maître d'Hôtel 116
Roasted Sweet Potato Mash 204
Rognons d'Agneau à la Diable 146

S

salads
- Curly Endive Salad with Bacon & Poached Egg 193
- Liver, Spinach & Bacon Salad with Mustard Vinaigrette 198
- Peppered Porterhouse Salad 189
- Pistachio Sausage & Potato Salad 192
- A Salad in the Style of Lyon 188
- A Salad in the Style of Nice with Fresh Tuna 190
- Tolarno's Caesar Salad 197
- Tomato Salad 194

Salade Aixoise 196
Salade de Céleri-rave 18
Salade Frisée aux Lardons et Oeufs Pochés 193
Salade Lyonnaise 188
Salade Niçoise 190
Salade Nouvelle 198
Salade de Saucisson Pistache et Pommes de Terre 192
Salade de Tomates 194

sauces
- Béarnaise Sauce 170
- Black Pepper & Lemon-spiked Sauce 141
- Green Peppercorn Sauce 166
- Hollandaise Sauce 53
- Lobster Sauce 114
- Mornay Sauce 257
- Orange Sauce 97
- Sauce Gribiche 60
- Tartare Sauce 256

Sauerkraut in the Style of Alsace 181
Saumon Grillé et Sauce Vierge 119

sausages
- Freshly Shucked Oysters with Spicy Sausages 20
- Pistachio Sausage & Potato Salad 192
- A Salad in the Style of Lyon 188
- Sauerkraut in the Style of Alsace 181
- Tagine of Duck Confit, Lamb Kefta & Merguez Sausage in Harissa Broth 98
- Toulouse Sausages with Lentil & Cabbage Stew 178

Sautéed Chicken with Tarragon 94
Sautéed Potatoes with Onions 213
Sautéed Veal with Lemon 133

scallops
- Scallops in the Style of Provence 104
- Zucchini Flowers Stuffed with a Scallop Mousseline 61

seafood
- Blue Swimmer Crabs in the Bouillabaisse Style 110
- Cheese Gratinéed Lobster in Mustard Cream 109
- Cheese Gratinéed Seafood Crepes 112
- Freshly Shucked Oysters with Spicy Sausages 20
- Garlic Prawns 113
- Lobster Soufflé 49
- Mussels in the Portuguese Style 108
- Mussels in a White Wine Broth 106
- Prawn Cocktail 50
- Roasted Moreton Bay Bugs with Beurre Maître d'Hôtel 116
- Scallop Mousseline 61
- Scallops in the Style of Provence 104
- A Seafood Stew with Garlic Mayonnaise 105
- Zucchini Flowers Stuffed with a Scallop Mousseline 61

Shepherd's Pie 135
Shortcrust Pastry 52
Slow-cooked Shredded Pork Pâté in its Own Fat 31
Slow-roasted Onions With Olive Oil & Wine Vinegar 204
Slow-roasted Tomatoes on Sourdough with Feta 58

smoked salmon
- Potato Blini with Smoked Salmon & Salmon Caviar 65
- Potted Smoked Salmon 25

Snails in Garlic Butter 48
Snapper with Pistou Mash, Parmesan & Brown Butter 124
Snow Eggs 232
Snow Pea Soup with a Splash of Champagne 73

soufflés
- Cappuccino Soufflé 239
- Lobster Soufflé 49
- Twice Baked Cheese Soufflés 61

Soufflé de Homard 49
Soufflés à la Suissesse 61

soups
- Cheese Gratinéed French Onion Soup 73
- Chilled Leek & Potato Soup 72
- Cream of Carrot Soup 68
- The Farmer's Vegetable Soup 76
- A Hearty Winter Soup from the Basque Region 69
- A Provençal Vegetable Soup with Basil 70
- Snow Pea Soup with a Splash of Champagne 73

Soupe Cultivateur 76
Soupe à l'Oignon Gratinée 73
Soupe de Panais au Cari 76
Soupe au Pistou 70
A Specialty from Aix-en-Provence 196
spinach
    Creamed Spinach 200
    Eggs on a Plate with Spinach 64
    Liver, Spinach & Bacon Salad with Mustard Vinaigrette 198
    Lobster & Spinach Quenelles with Lobster Sauce 114–15
    Tongue, Pork & Spinach Terrine 28
Steak Tartare with Parmesan & Garlic Toasts 165
stews
    Brain, Yabbie & Sweetbread Stew 145
    Lentil & Cabbage Stew 178
    Provençal Beef Stew 164
    A Provençal Vegetable Stew with a Poached Egg 66
    A Seafood Stew with Garlic Mayonnaise 105
    Spiced Tomato, Capsicum & Potato Stew 122
    White Veal Stew with Onions & Mushrooms 137
stocks
    Beef Stock 254
    Chicken Stock 254
    Fish Stock 255
    Vegetable Stock 254
sweet potato
    Roasted Sweet Potato Mash 204
sweetbreads
    Brain, Yabbie & Sweetbread Stew 145

T

Tagine of Duck Confit, Lamb Kefta & Merguez Sausage in Harissa Broth 98
Tartare Sauce 256

tarts
    French Apple Tart 234
    Leek & Cheese Tart 52
    Lemon Tart 244
    Poached Pear Tart 249
Tarte au Citron 244
Tarte aux Pommes 234
terrines
    The Chef's Pork, Veal & Liver Terrine 33
    Jellied Oxtail Terrine 27
    Tongue, Pork & Spinach Terrine 28
Terrine du Chef 33
Terrine de Langue, Porc et Épinards 28
La Terrine de Queue de Boeuf 27
Thon Marmitako 122
Tian Provençal 206
The Tolarno Burger 174
Tolarno's Caesar Salad 197
tomatoes
    Braised Chicken with Capsicum, Pancetta & Tomato 93
    Eggplant, Onion & Tomato Gratin 206
    Gratinéed Tomatoes 208
    Slow-roasted Tomatoes on Sourdough with Feta 58
    Spiced Tomato, Capsicum & Potato Stew 122
    Tomato Chutney 258
    Tomato, Fresh Herb & Lemon Oil 119
    Tomato Salad 194
Tomates à la Provençale 208
tongue
    Ox Tongue with Herb Mayonnaise 148
    Tongue, Pork & Spinach Terrine 28
Toulouse Sausages with Lentil & Cabbage Stew 178
Tournedos au Poivre Vert 166
Tripe & Onions in the Style of Lyon 149
Tripes à la Lyonnaise 149
Trout with Almonds 121

Truite aux Amandes 121
tuna
    A Salad in the Style of Nice with Fresh Tuna 190
    Tuna with a Spiced Tomato, Capsicum & Potato Stew 122
Twice Baked Cheese Soufflés 61

V

veal
    The Chef's Pork, Veal & Liver Terrine 33
    Home-style Veal Shanks 138
    Parmesan-crumbed Veal with Dubonnet & Orange 136
    Sautéed Veal with Lemon 133
    White Veal Stew with Onions & Mushrooms 137
vegetables
    The Farmer's Vegetable Soup 76
    A Provençal Vegetable Soup with Basil 70
    A Provençal Vegetable Stew with a Poached Egg 66
    Vegetable Stock 254
    see also particular vegetables
vinaigrette
    Mustard Vinaigrette 257

W

White Veal Stew with Onions & Mushrooms 137
Whiting Fillets with Lemon Butter 125
Wholemeal Bread 35

Y

yabbies
    Brain, Yabbie & Sweetbread Stew 145
yoghurt
    Cherry Yoghurt Ice-cream 246

Z

Zucchini Flowers Stuffed with a Scallop Mousseline 61

Picture Credits

All photography is by Greg Elms, except where detailed below.

From Mirka Mora's personal collection: pages 4, 7, 8, 11 and 15

From Iain Hewitson's personal collection: page 9 (bottom right)

From the Herald and Weekly Times archive: pages 78, 81 (top and bottom)

From the La Trobe Picture Collection, State Library of Victoria: page 9, 'Fitzroy Street, St Kilda', courtesy of Rose Stereograph Co; page 41, 'Tolarno', circa 1940-60, courtesy of Rose Stereograph Co; page 41, postcard of Fitzroy St, St Kilda, circa 1912

Courtesy Port Phillip City Collection: plans of Tolarno, pages 42–45

Courtesy of Serge Thomann: page 251 (photograph taken on 26 May 2006,

the last Friday at Tolarno Bistro)

The artwork used on the case of the book is reproduced with the permission of Mirka Mora, and is a detail from one of her paintings in the hallway at Tolarno. The back jacket and endpaper photographs were taken in the last days of Tolarno Bistro.